All About Dog Daycare
... A Blueprint For Success

Robin K. Bennett, CPDT

C&R Publishing, LLC ~ Woodbridge, Virginia

All About Dog Daycare . . . A Blueprint For Success
By Robin K. Bennett, CPDT

Published by:
C&R Publishing, LLC
Post Office Box 4227
Woodbridge VA 22194-4227 USA
info@allaboutdogdaycare.com
www.allaboutdogdaycare.com

Bennett, Robin
All About Dog Daycare...A Blueprint For Success/
Robin Bennett, CPDT

P.cm.
Includes index
ISBN 1-933562-52-8
1. Small Business 2. Entrepreneurship

Cover by Brier Design
Front Cover photos: Top photo by Maureen Daniels
                       Middle photo by Lawrence Giberson
                       Bottom photo by Robin Bennett
Rear Cover photo by Michael Woodward

All other photos courtesy of the author with the following exceptions:
Michael Woodward (p. iv, 94, 95, 182); Kim Kirilenko (p. 6); Janet Galante (p.20); Gary Bessette (p. 54); Lisa Crigger (p. 55); Dawn Walton (p. 55)

BOOK / ROTH
16.27

Acknowledgements

Writing a book is a task involving many people beyond the person listed on the book cover. This book is no different.

A word of thanks to the many trainers, entrepreneurs, friends and family members who read and edited the various chapters of this book: Annette Ahtes, Cindy Briggs (who graciously offered her time to me when I first opened my daycare), Susan Briggs, Cindy Bruckart, Diana Craig, Stacy Dempsey, Anna Doell, Roz Ferber, Susan Ferry, Jim Krack, Don Knepp, Ron Knepp (who supplied countless title suggestions), Michele Knepp (who supplied countless additional title suggestions), Dr. Debby Loveland, JulieRae MacLeod, Marilyn Marks, Kathy Minnick, Penny Munaro, Susan McCullough, Bob Payne, Colleen Pelar, Caroline Roden, Laura Sharkey, Pat Sinclair, Jamie Smelser, Dawn Walton, Charlene Woodward (for providing support from the publishing world) and Miranda Workman. A special thank you to the staff at Starbucks Coffee® in Stafford, Virginia for allowing me to occupy a table for long periods of time while writing this book. The mochas kept me going.

To those families who trusted me with their dogs in my daycare. You and your dogs have been wonderful teachers and I'm thankful for the opportunity to learn from you.

To the wonderful and amazing staff at my own training facility, All About Dogs, Inc.: Keely Bovais, Diana Craig, AnnMarie Dykes, Denise Frano, Roz Ferber, Eileen Fulk, Mary Graham, Chris Johnson, Kim Kirilenko, Colleen Pelar, Vicky Shields-Harding, Julie Fudge Smith, and Martha Walker. It is an honor to work with each one of you, and I truly appreciate your friendships. Thank you for everything you do.

To my parents, Don and Alice Knepp, for their constant support in everything I've chosen to do....even when the idea was a bit crazy.

A special word of thanks to my dad for his conscientious, *green, felt-tip pen* editing of my high school papers. Your careful work when I was younger has given me the confidence to write (despite what I may have said during high school!)

Finally, thank you to my own family. To my husband, Greg, for giving me all the time I needed to work on my book and supporting me through the tremendously busy periods. Thanks also to my kids, Leanna and Nathan, who enthusiastically supported the entire book from start to finish even when it meant they couldn't go to the pool. I love you all very much.

Owning and operating a dog daycare is an incredible job and a tremendous responsibility. Remember to have fun, but take good care of the dogs.

~Robin Knepp Bennett

Please feel free to contact me with any questions or suggestions you have regarding this book or the dog daycare industry. I look forward to hearing from you.

Robin@allaboutdogdaycare.com
PO Box 4227
Woodbridge, VA 22194

Table of Contents

Chapter 1:
Introduction

PET SERVICE INDUSTRY GROWTH

Each year, Americans become more and more willing to purchase upscale services and care for their pets. Between 1996 – the year I started my first dog daycare facility – and 2005, American pet owners have boosted their pet budgets by nearly 75 percent; this year, the American Pet Product Manufacturers Association (APPMA) predicts owners will shell out nearly $36 billion to care for their animal friends. This growth is projected to continue.

At the same time, families are working longer hours and struggling constantly to find a balance between family needs and work requirements. These struggles have boosted demand for service-oriented businesses.

> ### Pet owners will spend approximately
> ### thirty-six billion dollars on their pets in 2005
> ### ~APPMA

Meanwhile, the Humane Society of the United States (HSUS) estimates that more than one-third of U.S. households now own at least one dog. These dogs have moved from the back yard dog house straight into the family living rooms and even bedrooms. They have become full family members who provide companionship and health benefits to humans. But while people want to have dogs, they

often feel guilty when their busy lives prevent them from spending enough quality time with their pets.

In response to owners' busy lifestyles and the increased desire to pamper their pets, dog daycare facilities have sprung up all over the country. Dog-loving entrepreneurs have an exciting opportunity to combine their love of animals with a money-making enterprise.

Approximately one-third of all households in the United States own at least one dog ~HSUS

WHAT IS DOG DAYCARE?

Dog daycare is a new term in society. Its meaning has not been standardized, and consumers and entrepreneurs would benefit from understanding the various uses.

This book uses the term *dog daycare* specifically to describe a supervised environment in which dogs play off-leash with other dogs. Like child daycare centers, a dog daycare center caters to busy dog parents who want to provide their dog with exercise and playtime. The daycare provides the dog with a fun, safe, stimulating environment during the day while owners shop, run errands, or work. The daycare business is responsible for ensuring the safety of the dogs in their care and making sure all the dogs play nicely together. Also like child daycare centers, dog daycare facilities usually include a caring, compassionate staff; plenty of safe, fun playground equipment; and often, snack and naptimes for the dogs in their care.

Dog daycare differs significantly from day boarding, in which a dog is crated or kenneled during the daytime hours. For the purposes of this book, such services do not constitute dog daycare. Dog daycare, as discussed here, refers to facilities

that allow dogs to play together off-leash and are an alternative to boarding a dog in a crate, kennel or run. Although dog daycares may crate or kennel dogs during short periods of time (for instance in order to feed the dogs), the dogs spend most of the day playing and interacting with other dogs.

Dog daycare must also be distinguished from field trips or pet sitting services in which a dog can play with another dog for 30 to 45 minutes. Dog daycare services are usually day-long or at least several hours long.

A dog daycare provides owners with a safe, fun, stimulating environment for their dog to play off-leash with other dogs under the careful supervision of a trained staff

The benefits of a dog daycare are numerous. First of all, the dogs learn how to play with other dogs and increase their social skills. Second, dogs use up a great deal of energy during their time at daycare, which makes for a well-rested pet in the evening. Rather than coming home to a hyper dog who has been alone all day, owners will pick up an exhausted dog whose low energy level matches the owners. Third, dog daycare helps alleviate behavior problems. Trainers agree the vast majority of behavior problems (for example excessive barking, chewing and digging) - particularly in puppies - result from lack of exercise. Dog daycare centers address this problem by giving dogs the opportunity to play. Finally, owners have peace of mind knowing their dog will be well cared for and well-exercised throughout the day; it allows for guilt-free dog ownership.

IS DAYCARE THE RIGHT BUSINESS FOR ME?

Owning and operating a daycare is not easy, but you are more likely to succeed if you plan your business carefully. Start by ensuring you have the skills and finances to be successful.

Business Skills

First and foremost, a daycare owner needs to have some basic business management and organizational skills before embarking on this venture. According to the Small Business Administration about 80 percent of all new businesses fail within the first five years. This failure often results from a new owner's lack of business management skills. If you are starting a new business, you need to be able to set a plan, stick to it, adapt as necessary, and work unsupervised. You also need to be self motivated and have an appetite for hard work. The ability to dream is one thing; the ability to make that dream come true is another. See appendix B for resources that can help you start your new business.

Animal Skills

Daycare owners and their employees need to understand how dogs behave when they interact with other dogs off-leash. This understanding needs to go beyond basic knowledge of what dogs look like when they are acting aggressive or fearful. There are numerous warning signals and subtle body cues you need to learn when dealing with dogs in a group environment. These signals and cues are your key to preventing fights, to knowing which dogs will play well and which will not, and for keeping the dogs safe. Mistakes or misunderstandings can result in injury or death to a dog entrusted to your daycare's service.

Do not practice with other people's dogs. Acquire this knowledge before you open your dog daycare. Visit dog parks, off-leash playgroups, or any facility where dogs can freely play with other dogs to learn how to read dogs so you will be better able to supervise and control a group of dogs. Chapter 6 deals extensively with understanding canine behavior.

You also need to understand how dogs think and learn. This understanding enables you to prevent unwanted behaviors in the daycare environment, such as jumping or barking, from starting or from continuing. Such knowledge will also help you teach the dogs how to calm down and otherwise help you resolve problems in the daycare environment.

People Skills

Daycare owners also need good communications skills and the ability to deal with a wide range of personalities. Would-be daycare owners often overlook this requirement if they enter the industry because they like animals better than people. Although daycare owners spend most of the day dealing only with dogs, all those dogs have moms and dads who want assurance that you are providing the best possible care to their pet. These dog parents are the daycare's real clients, and you need strong people skills to communicate effectively and efficiently with them. In addition, you will need to deal with the media, local veterinarians, and other pet professionals, some of whom may not like or even understand what dog daycare is.

Money

Finally, you need to have enough money to support yourself during their initial period of growth (and enough energy to survive this period). Based on my experience, the average daycare requires a minimum of two years before it generates a significant profit. During this growth stage, you will be breathing, eating, and sleeping your daycare plan.

The average daycare requires a minimum
of two years before it generates
a significant profit.

Expect to work long hours, get little rest, and spend a great deal of money for at least the first two years. Your family also needs to be able to handle this period of stress when you are putting forth a great deal of effort and receiving little or no monetary reward.

THE JOYS OF OWNING A DAYCARE

Owning a daycare can be very rewarding. A daycare business offers plenty of excitement and variety, particularly when compared with typical 9-5 office jobs. You can get incredible enjoyment from meeting a wide variety of social, fun-loving animals and their owners.

The daycare clients you will encounter are amazing and diverse, but linked by a shared devotion to their dogs. Your clients will share their worries, concerns, and joys with you and the rest of the daycare staff as you become a part of their extended family.

Two puppies meet for the first time

Once your business is established, you will receive the flexibility and freedom to set your own schedule and work as much (or as little) as you like. Indeed, this is often the main reason people want to start their own businesses.

THE RISKS OF OWNING A DAYCARE

First and foremost is the risk of failure; a risk all entrepreneurs face. Failure in a daycare could mean the business did not succeed financially – or worse, that a dog was hurt or killed while in your care. Hopefully, with the information contained in this book and through the references provided, you will minimize such risks.

Another risk is having your heart broken when dogs and clients you grow to love get hurt, reach old age or must cross the Rainbow Bridge. You will miss them terribly and grieve with the families.

Finally, owning a dog daycare carries a huge risk of burnout. Though you will be extremely busy, especially the first two years, your free time needs to be preciously planned and viciously guarded to prevent burnout, which can prevent you from reaching your dream.

WHAT IS IN THIS BOOK

This book is geared toward new entrepreneurs who wish to start their own dog daycares as well as veterinarians, dog trainers, behaviorists, kennel operators, pet sitters, and other animal care specialists who may be interested in expanding their current business to include daycare. In addition, current daycare owners will find that this book will help them improve their operations and train new staff members. Policies and procedures outlined in this book will help keep dogs and staff members safe as they interact in a unique setting and will clarify what daycare owners and employees should expect of one another.

Appendix A contains sample forms and documents you can use in the daily operation of your daycare. Appendix B is a compilation of contact and resource information for daycare businesses.

The joys of owning and operating your own daycare far outweigh the risks for the motivated, dog-loving entrepreneur. Let me help you plan and prepare as you embark upon your dream.

Plan to embark upon your dream...

Chapter 2:
Getting Started

Before you actually open your daycare, you need to create a business plan – and before you create a business plan, you need to make some decisions about what kind of daycare operation you want to run. This chapter provides *food for thought* as you begin planning your facility.

TYPE OF DAYCARE

The type of daycare you establish will result from your decisions about size, location, and staffing. These decisions will influence your business plan and profitability as well.

Small Dogs, Large Dogs, or Both?

Some daycares accept dogs of all sizes, while others accept only dogs within a certain weight limit. If you accept dogs of all sizes, you will need to have separate areas for large and small dogs. Regardless of how well individual large dogs and small dogs play together, the risk of injury rises when you put the two groups together. By creating separate play areas, you can put appropriately sized dogs together and minimize the risk of injury. Of course, different play areas require increased staffing because you may need more people to watch multiple play areas. Chapter 6 includes information on dog behavior and guidelines for separating the dogs.

Puppies, Adults, or Both?

As with size, the ages of the dogs in daycare may affect the layout of the play areas. Puppies 5 months and under need their own play area until they are big enough to *run with the*

big dogs. Daycare provides a wonderful socialization experience for puppies, and proper socialization can prevent many behavior problems. However, puppies need constant monitoring to ensure they are not overwhelmed or scared by other dogs. The negative impact of one bad experience can stay with the affected puppy for the rest of his life.

If you are going to accept puppies, at what age will they be allowed to attend? There is an inherent risk of disease with a very young puppy. However, this risk can be minimized by ensuring the puppy is receiving adequate care, vaccinations, and nutrition during his first few months. Many daycares accept puppies into daycare as young as 12 weeks as long as the pups are healthy and have received at least two sets of puppy vaccinations.

Dogs over 5 years of age prefer a slower activity level than the average adolescent. If you accept dogs over 5 years old, consider having a small room where they can rest with other dogs of similar energy levels.

PUPPY DAYCARE?

When I first started my daycare, I assumed it would be for puppies age 5 months and younger. As a trainer, I understood the benefit of and highly encouraged early socialization. All my advertising efforts, including signs, business cards and flyers said *All About Dogs, Professional Dog Training and Puppy Daycare*. Little did I realize the majority of my dogs would be adolescent dogs between the ages of 6 months and 2 years. Be careful when you make assumptions about what you think your clients will need. Their true needs may be differ from what you expect.

Neutering/Spaying

Will you require dogs to be neutered/spayed? If so, at what age will you prohibit them from attending daycare if they are

not neutered or spayed? Will you deal with any clients who show or breed their dogs? Answering these questions will help you formulate your neuter/spay policy.

Most daycares require a dog to be neutered or spayed by 7 months of age in order to attend daycare. There are clear benefits to this policy. First, you encourage responsible pet ownership by recommending a neuter/spay policy. Second, you reduce the chance of an accidental mating. Finally, you make your employee's job a little easier and safer because the staff does not have to deal with any hormone-related behavior issues.

Obviously, if you accept intact males and females, you will need a policy to ensure females in heat are prohibited from attending daycare. There is some controversy over whether or not you accept a higher risk of aggression due to hormone changes in the dogs that are not neutered or spayed. You can minimize any risk by having strict screening policies for all dogs.

Breed Restrictions
Will you accept all breed as long as they pass your screening assessment or restrict certain breeds? What about wolf-hybrids? There are pros and cons to any breed restriction in a daycare setting. In some areas of the country, wolf-hybrids are illegal. Sometimes, if a wolf-hybrid bites another person or dog, the state or county may not accept the rabies vaccination and may require the immediate disposal of the animal and treatment of the victim with rabies treatment. If this is the case in your county/state, you have a good justification for prohibiting wolf-hybrids in your daycare.

Some breeds may be more difficult than others to manage in the high energy, group situation of a daycare. Some dogs require a greater level of supervision to ensure the safety of the group. You will need to determine if your staffing goals will allow you to accept all breeds or restrict certain breeds. You will also need to check with your insurance company to

ensure they do not impose any breed restrictions to your dog daycare insurance coverage.

WHAT ABOUT AMERICAN PIT BULL AND STAFFORDSHIRE TERRIERS?

Two breeds receiving a great deal of discussion among daycare owners are the American Pit Bull Terrier and the American Staffordshire Terrier. Some daycares accept these breeds based on an individual assessment of each dog. Based on my experience with daycares located in large metropolitan areas, these breeds are very easily aroused and play roughly in the average daycare setting.

Arousal in dogs (a general state of excitement, agitation or stress) is a contributing factor to aggression. The more activity and arousal you have in a group of dogs, the more likely you are to have a fight. These breeds go from playing to fighting very quickly and are challenging for your staff to monitor in a group. If your staff is new or has limited canine body language observation skills in a group setting, you may want to reduce your risk of problems by restricting these breeds in your daycare. American Staffordshire Terriers and American Pit Bull Terriers often do better in smaller, less active groups than in large, excitable groups and require incredibly close supervision to ensure they do not get too aroused while at the daycare. For more information on canine behavior, see chapter 6.

Other Services

Will your daycare provide additional services to clients? There are a wide range of services you can offer as a means of increasing your business revenue – but you need to plan for them beforehand. When planning your facility, be sure to consider not only where you will perform the additional services, but also how you will move dogs between areas. For example, if you offer grooming, be sure you do not have to move the dogs to be groomed through the play areas to reach the grooming station.

ADDITIONAL SERVICES TO CONSIDER

Overnight boarding
Pet sitting
Daytime boarding (for dogs that cannot play with
    daycare dogs but need a place to stay during the
    day)
One-on-one play time and interaction
Daily outings or special walks (field trips)
Training
Grooming
Nail trimming
Massage
Tellington Touch
Acupuncture
Transportation Services to/from the owner's home or
    veterinarian

Clients can pay an additional fee for any extra services
or the costs of these services can be included in the price of
your daycare.

WHO ARE YOUR CLIENTS?

The typical daycare client earns a middle-to-high income (often as part of a duel-income family) and works long or irregular hours. Usually, the main decision makers for dogs in daycare are the women of the house. Many clients have no children because they are either younger and are delaying a family or they are older and the children have grown. For daycare clients, their pets are their children and they are spending a great deal of disposable income on their child. The daycare clients consider daycare an important part of their dog's lives. Clients will pay heavily for excellent service and care for their pet.

Beyond those generalities, the make-up of your local community will drive some of your decisions about what type of daycare you will provide. For example, if you live in a city full of high-rise condominiums and apartments with a great

deal of smaller dogs, a small-dog daycare may be ideal. If your client base contains a large number of breeders or individuals participating in conformation shows, then you may want to loosen your neutering/spaying policies.

You want to know about your clients for advertising purposes. As an example, if the majority of your clients are women, advertising in the sports section of the local newspaper would not be beneficial.

MARKET RESEARCH

Before you get started, you may be inclined to conduct market research analysis. For established industries, market research can provide a methodical approach to choosing the right target market for any given product or service. The target markets are determined by comparing similar businesses offering similar services.

At this time, the dog daycare industry is still relatively new and very few market research studies are available to help you determine if your research matches any normal standard for the industry. You may be able to obtain county animal licensing information and make estimates on the number of dogs in your area as compared to nationwide figures. For reviewing general market assumptions, refer to some of the business planning references located in appendix B.

One relatively simple assessment of probability of success for a daycare is a quick review of other dog-related industries in your area. In particular, a high number of veterinarians within a small radius of successful daycares is common. I have seen 16 to 30 veterinarians within a 5 to 10 mile radius of some very successful daycare facilities. Until a more formal market research methodology has evolved, review all these ideas to determine if a dog daycare will be successful in your area.

PARTNERING WITH OTHER PET SERVICES

If you do not offer all services, consider recommending a nearby facility in return for them advertising the services of your business. Here are some possibilities:

- Consider hiring a mobile groomer to come to your facility every 4 to 6 weeks to groom daycare dogs.
- Provide transportation to a nearby boarding facility that can keep the dog overnight. The client would pay your daycare for daytime play activity and transportation while the boarding facility receives payment for overnight boarding.
- Work with a local pet sitting company that might be interested in conducting transportation services to your clients.

These sorts of partnerships can be very lucrative and are a win-win situation for both businesses.

LOCATING A SPACE FOR YOUR DAYCARE

Once you know what type of daycare you want, you need to think about a space. The assumptions you made in determining the type of daycare you will operate, the services you will offer and the market for your business will help determine the size and location of your facility. You will look for a space at the same time you write your business plan. Business plans are discussed later in this chapter.

This phase of daycare development can often be the most time consuming and frustrating. You will face numerous questions and issues such as zoning and other community restrictions. The lack of formalized statutes for daycares will require patience and perseverance on your part as you research your options and deal with local government officials. The next section addresses some of these issues.

RENT OR OWN

Do you want to rent or own your new daycare facility? There is obviously less financial risk involved in renting a facility unless you already own a suitable building. Generally speaking, space for a warehouse will cost less per square foot than space in a retail center. A commercial real estate agent can provide you with an idea of average rent costs in your area because it will vary considerably from county to county and state to state.

It is beyond the scope of this book to provide specific information on lease negotiation. However, a few simple facts are provided to get you started.

Rent costs are often specified on an annual cost per square foot amount. To determine the monthly cost, simply multiply the square footage by the cost per square foot, and divide that figure by 12. For instance, if a 1600 square foot building is renting for $18 per square foot, you will multiply 1600 by 18 dollars, which equals $28,800 per year. By dividing $28,800 by 12 months, you determine your monthly rent will cost $2400. Plan on paying an upfront deposit equal to one months rent when you sign the lease.

Retail space is usually quoted as a cost for rent and does not include common area maintenance (CAM) costs, insurance costs (paid to the landlord), or taxes (also paid to the landlord). Be sure to ask for monthly charges for CAM, taxes, and insurance when you are working to determine your monthly payments for a retail location because these costs can often add hundreds of dollars to your monthly rental fee.

Warehouse spaces are usually quoted as *triple net*, which will include insurance, taxes, and maintenance costs. For both retail and warehouse locations, be sure to ask who is responsible for utilities and what annual expenses can be expected, if any.

NEGOTIATING A LEASE

Always read the fine print. Most leases are mountainous documents and need to be reviewed in their entirety. In general, the longer the term of the lease, the better negotiating power you have with the landlord. The landlord wants to keep the space rented as long as possible and will work harder to establish a long term commitment. A 3-year lease will offer you little room to negotiate while a 10-year lease will give you plenty of room to bargain. Keep in mind that all provisions in the lease are negotiable. Here are some helpful tips for the first time business owner:

- Consider keeping lease payments low during the first few months when you will be doing construction or will have very little business because you just opened. Landlords may be willing to give you 1 to 3 months of free rent or ½ price rent to ease your budget a little.
- Negotiate leasehold improvements and cut down costs of your own construction by including them in work the landlord will do for you before your occupancy.
- If you need several months to do construction, try to negotiate a lease commencement date (when you start paying rent) that will begin after the lease signing date. If possible, make this date flexible in case construction delays occur. If not, contract with your construction company to hold them accountable for lease payments that become due if you are not open due to their negligence or delays.
- Make sure you include a lease clause that allows you to get out of the lease without penalty if you are unable to obtain zoning or occupancy due to country restrictions that are out of your control.

SIZE

The size of your daycare depends on what you can afford, what the market will bear, and what your goals are. Generally speaking, you can estimate a space requirement of 70 to 100 square feet per dog, depending on the size of the dog. Keep in mind that your break-even point depends on the number of dogs in daycare and the amount charged per dog, minus your

expenses. For example, if you determine you will need 25 dogs at $20 a day in order to break even, you need a space that is at least 1750-2500 square feet. If your space is not large enough, you may not be able to keep 25 dogs safely. These numbers will be important when you begin your business plan.

Estimate 70 to 100 square feet of play area per dog, depending on the size of the dog

Once you determine the size of the play area, remember to add space needed for storage, a bathroom, an office and/or lobby area as well as an area where there is adequate room for evaluating the dogs for daycare. You will also need to include space required for any additional services you will offer. Chapter 4 discusses how to set up a daycare facility.

LOCATION, LOCATION, LOCATION

Typically, most successful daycare centers are located in a central, easy-to-access area. Because the daycare client is looking for a safe, fun place for his dog to play, any town or city in which houses without yards are prevalent (i.e., suburbs with small lots, condominiums, townhouses, apartments, etc.) or where dogs have no place to play are good choices for a daycare. If this location is coupled with a working environment where owners usually work long hours due to local industry standards (i.e. film industry personnel in California) or have long commutes (i.e. workers commuting to Washington, D.C., in Northern Virginia), you have increased your odds of finding a good location for a daycare.

Locate your daycare where it is easy to reach from major streets of the city. However, your location will depend, at least in part, on local zoning regulations and the cost to lease or rent the space.

DAYCARE FROM YOUR HOME?

It is possible to operate a dog daycare from your home. However, zoning regulations often prevent your doing so. Before starting your home daycare, be sure to get compliance from local neighbors as well as your zoning office. Your home, as well as your yard, will suffer damage which may result in a lower resale value of your home. Your neighbors can file complaints to shut down the daycare even if you are properly zoned for the business.

ZONING

Local zoning ordinances vary within every county and state. Zoning controls the type of businesses a community will allow to open within various parts of the city. Simply put, zoning dictates where you can do business and what type of business you can do. Most counties and states have several types of zoning codes. Examples are a code for retail services with a list of what services constitutes a retail business; a code for agricultural or industrial zoning with specific definitions on what constitutes such enterprises; and residential zoning with a list permissible home-based businesses.

Why is zoning important? If your daycare is zoned as a retail business (such as a pet store), you have a greater chance of operating near a residential area, but will probably be prohibited from boarding dogs overnight. If you are zoned as an agricultural business (such as a kennel), you may need to operate in a warehouse or industrial location off the beaten path and will probably rely more heavily upon marketing and signage for advertising (at least in the beginning).

When you begin your search for a dog daycare center, you will usually be looking at warehouse and retail spaces. Generally speaking, the warehouse-type spaces will be farther from main streets. Retail locations, on the other hand, usually offer great access to main sections of the city and good

visibility, but are often more costly. In any location, though, you will need to address the concerns of the landlord and possible neighbors about dog activities in the building. As you look at possible locations you will need to familiarize yourself with local zoning regulations. All these factors are important to your business plan because rent varies considerably between retail locations and warehouses. In addition you may plan a different marketing campaign if you are not located in a heavily trafficked retail location.

Warehouses can be painted to look fun and inviting

You may be able to obtain special permits to allow you to place a commercially zoned business in a residential retail area, but this often requires extensive community debates, time and money.

OCCUPANCY

Once you have your zoning approval, you will begin to work on the facility layout and design and other construction issues. Chapter 4 discusses layout and design considerations for the daycare. Before you actually begin building, you will need to have plans drawn up for most construction projects, particularly if they involve electrical or plumbing work.

These plans will need approval from your county government office, both before and after the work is done. Once all the work is complete and your facility has been inspected for compliance with all country permit offices and the fire marshal, you will receive a certificate of occupancy and can begin operating your facility. Work with your local government office to determine how long the approval process takes.

COMMUNITY CONCERNS

Do not assume that just because your neighboring tenant is an auto-body shop the community will allow a dog daycare facility. Landlord and community concerns over dog daycare facilities are one obstacle you need to address to the satisfaction of all complaining parties (many of whom are not dog lovers). Some common reasons communities and landlords do not want a dog daycare include, but are not limited to: excessive noise, excessive odors, rat infestations, unsightly ground coverings, spread of infectious disease within the community, germs spread through dog feces, and environmental hazards. Most of these complaints are not realistic problems faced by a well-run dog daycare. However, you need to address them professionally and explain how you will prevent them from occurring.

STAFFING AND HOURS

These two items go hand-in-hand because they are instrumental in determining your break-even point. The more hours you are open, the larger your staff may need to be. Ideally, your on-site staff-to-dog ratio will be one person to every 10 to 15 dogs, depending on the sizes of the dogs and the experience of the staff member.

Some daycares do not supervise the dogs constantly or use TV monitors to watch the dogs. Such practices are very dangerous because the staff has no control over the group play environment and cannot intervene quickly if problems arise.

WHY IS IT SO HARD TO GET A DAYCARE ZONED?

At this time, very few states and counties have any zoning specifically for dog daycares. If you are the first daycare in your community, you will often face obstacles in getting any zoning for your business because none may exist. You will usually face complaints by the community, which need to be satisfactorily defused. (See box entitled Community Concerns). It is not uncommon for the zoning process to run for months or even years depending on the individual zoning office.

If you know where you would like to open your facility, find out how that location is zoned and determine if there are pet-related industries allowed in that type of zoned area. If so, try to approach the zoning office to show why your business fits definitions similar to an industry already allowed.

When I opened my daycare, the zoning office wanted to zone it as a kennel and limit me to industrial areas. I did not offer overnight boarding (the county definition of a kennel) and wanted to be located in a shopping center. After researching the pet industries allowed in a shopping center, I discovered that pet stores are zoned for retail and allowed in shopping centers. Because I sold some pet supplies for my training classes, I approached the zoning office and explained that, in addition to offering daycare, I also sold pet supplies. The zoning office zoned my business as a pet store and allowed me to operate the daycare in a shopping center.

I ry to work with the zoning office to meet its requirements and keep a cool head during the sometimes long and tedious process. The county officials are doing their jobs, and you will need to work within their rules in order to get your daycare open.

The staff-to-dog ratio will be one person to every 10-15 dogs, depending on the size of the dogs and the experience of the staff member

Other daycares control the staffing needs by splitting dogs into two groups and allowing only half to play at any given time while the other half is crated. The two groups are switched throughout the day. This can reduce the staffing required, but will require more space to crate or house the dogs when they are not in the play environment. If you operate in this manner, your clients must clearly understand that their dogs will be spending as much time napping as they are playing.

Chapter 7 contains information on dog handling polices while chapter 5 contains detailed information on staff scheduling.

PAYROLL

Payroll often consumes 20 to 25 percent of the revenue in a well-run daycare – much higher than for most other businesses and a significant obstacle to generating a large profit in a dog daycare. The daycare industry is personnel intense. Providing close, on-hand supervision to a group of dogs will result in high payroll costs. Remember too, that customer service is very important in this business. You need well-trained, friendly staff members so the clients are happy to bring their beloved dog to your daycare - and, equally important, to recommend it to their friends. Cut expenses in other areas if necessary to ensure you have enough money to provide proper care and supervision for the dogs. Be sure to include an owner salary in your budget when figuring out your payroll expenses!

OTHER EXPENSES

In addition to the lease and payroll, you will need to make some general assumptions about other expenses required to operate your facility. These include utilities, equipment and supplies, payroll, taxes, legal fees, accounting fees, insurance, loan payments, postage, telephone, advertising, education, permits and dues and vehicle expense. Appendix B contains resources for companies that provide some of these services to dog daycare businesses.

Utilities
You will pay some or all of your utilities depending on your lease. Talking to other commercial businesses in your area will help you determine average monthly utility usage. Make sure you ask the landlord or neighboring tenants about variations in weather conditions and utility usage. If you have gas heat, your gas bill may be extremely low during the summer but could sky-rocket in the winter time. Understanding these adjustments will help you plan your budget.

Equipment/Supplies
You will need initial funds to equip your facility. After the initial set up, you will have routine monthly costs to keep your facility in stock with office and cleaning supplies. Prices will vary depending on the size of your facility and the type of services offered. Plan on an initial expense to set up your office and determine routine monthly fees to pay for restocking supplies. In your office supply budget, you may want to include the cost to operate your website and any internet access connections.

Taxes
You will need to pay federal, state, and possibly local taxes for your business. Tax payments will be paid on the income from daycare services and/or sales revenue as well as amounts paid for employee wages. An accountant can help you determine the costs for monthly, quarterly, and annual tax payments.

Legal/Accounting Fees
Legal counsel can review documents used in the set up of your daycare. For example, a real estate attorney can provide advice and guidance if you are uncomfortable reviewing lease documents. A certified public accountant, bookkeeper, or payroll service can handle your taxes and payroll payments if you are not prepared to determine these on your own. Expect to pay a minimum of a few hundred dollars annually for each of these services; in fact, most accountants may charge you

that amount per month for tax payments, bookkeeping services and monthly business statements.

Insurance

Expenses for insurance will usually average a few hundred dollars per month, but could be higher depending on the size of your facility and the services you provide. Coverage will include basic liability for your building to protect against normal hazards, disasters or maintenance issues. You will also need insurance to cover the dogs in your care. This insurance will normally cover the dogs as property and costs a few hundred dollars annually. Worker's compensation insurance is required by law for most companies with three or more employees. The rate you will pay will depend on the job each employee does. In general, you pay a fairly high rate for worker's compensation for dog daycare employees because their jobs entail more risk than that of a routine office worker. If you offer transportation services, you will also need insurance for company vehicles. Obtain bonding if you offer pet sitting or any other service that requires you to enter clients' homes.

Loan Payments

Remember to factor in any loan payments for vehicles, office equipment, or other business-related loans you have taken.

Postage

Postage fees will be needed for various forms, press releases, birthday cards, or other correspondence. Establishing a good website and using email correspondence will help keep your actual postage rates low. However, you may need to pay a monthly fee to the company or service provider that hosts your website.

FUNDING THE STARTUP OF YOUR COMPANY

Depending on the size of your daycare, the services you plan to offer, and the construction required in your facility, your startup costs could range from $15,000 to over $100,000. However, there are ways to raise these startup funds. Many daycare owners use their credit cards to get started. Another option is securing a personal or business loan. The Small Business Administration (SBA) offers loans to business. SBA loans are generally high risk to the SBA and therefore are high interest to the business. It is not uncommon to pay interest rates on an SBA loan that are 2-4% higher than that of a regular loan. Talk to your local bank for most affordable options that present you with as little risk and interest as possible. A well-written business plan including realistic growth potential is necessary to obtain any type of loan.

Telephone
Determine approximate costs for your business phone line, plus additional lines needed for fax machines and internet access. If you also need a cell phone, remember to include that expense as well. You may be able to reduce expenses by researching various business calling plans offered by phone and cable companies.

Advertising
As a general rule of thumb, plan on spending approximately 10 percent of your revenue for advertising. A comprehensive marketing plan will help you make the most of your advertising dollars. Investigate freebies, too. For example, press releases sent to all major newspaper, community papers and broadcast media can generate plenty of positive publicity – and it is free if you send your materials by email or fax. This type of free publicity can be very lucrative.

Education
Employee compensation can include benefits such as attendance at behavioral seminars. These benefits need to be

included in your business expenses. If you will attend annual conferences yourself, be sure to include costs to cover registration, hotel, travel, and food at the events.

Permits and Dues

Annual permits and licensing costs will include payments for vehicle registration, zoning permits, annual business licensing, and other state or federal permits required to operate your business. You may also want to include annual fees for membership in your local chamber of commerce and dues to professional organizations.

Vehicle Expenses

If you will use a vehicle for transportation you will need to budget for vehicle service, routine maintenance, insurance, repair, and fuel for the vehicle. Ensure you understand the rules in your state for tracking business vehicle expenses.

BUSINESS PLAN

Once you have made some overall assumptions about your daycare and have determined some basic costs for operating the facility, you can prepare a business plan. Your business plan will help you determine the estimated costs required to start your business and whether or not you will need outside funding. With your business expenses estimated, your business plan will also help you determine your break-even point and the fees to charge for services. Your business plan will help you to understand the length of time you can expect to be operating before your business in profitable and how soon you can reasonably expect to afford to offer each service you would like to provide. Several resources in appendix B offer advice on putting together a business plan.

For the average daycare owner, plan on operating for at least two years before reaching a significant profit point. This is especially true if you obtained a business loan or used your credit cards to get your business started.

SETTING PRICES

The price you set for your daycare and related services depends on the specific service being offered, your location and your competitor's prices. Most new business owners do not charge enough for their services initially. Check out the going rates in your area from other daycares, pet sitting services, and boarding facilities to get a general idea of what your market can bear. Clients will pay more for good quality service so charge more than your competitors if you are offering a better service.

Your business plan needs to be as accurate as possible. It is a living document that will fluctuate and change as you learn more about the daycare industry in your area. The old saying, "If you don't know where you are going, you won't know when you get there" is especially apt when creating a business plan. You need to have a goal in mind and adjust the goal with realistic expectations as your business grows and changes. A business plan helps you accomplish that and more.

OTHER BUSINESS CONCERNS

Now that you are well on your way to getting your business started, remember to consider a name for your company. Your local government and the U.S. Patent and Trademark Office are useful resources to help you determine whether the name you want to use is already being used by another business.

ESTIMATING DAYCARE GROWTH

One of the biggest challenges to preparing a realistic daycare business plan is making a good estimate of growth. As a new industry, daycare growth varies considerably. Most planners easily understand their break-even point as a description of cost per dog per day. For instance, if you have 20 dogs per day at a cost of $25 per dog, your business plan shows you will be able to pay all your expenses. In theory, it sounds easy to get 20 dogs in your daycare, right? This is a common misunderstanding among potential new owners.

There is a missing factor in terms of daycare growth: not all dogs will attend every day. Therefore, in order to get 20 dogs a day, you will need to estimate 5 to 7 times that number of actual clients. So, 20 dogs per day would equate to 100 to 140 different clients.

How fast will the daycare grow? For planning purposes, estimate approximately 2 to 3 new clients per week. Using this formula, you can see that getting 140 clients could take 11 to 18 months. No wonder it takes so long for most daycares to break even!

You will also want to determine your business entity. Several options for business entities exist including sole proprietorship, partnership, S corporation, C corporation, and limited liability company. Most daycare owners start out as sole proprietors, but end up changing their business entity for tax purposes when the company is generating more revenue. Work with your attorney and/or CPA to determine what entity is best for your personal and business financial liabilities.

A WORD ABOUT PERSONAL GUARANTEES

Many new dog daycare owners opt to set up their business as a corporation to protect their personal financial assets. While this is one good reason to establish a corporation, it is important to understand most new business owners, regardless of business entity, will be required to sign statements of personal guarantees for loans, vehicles, and leases. Unless you have owned a company before, and can prove yourself to be a low risk, you will be required to sign a personal guarantee before most agencies agree to do business with you. The personal guarantee negates any financial protection afforded to you by establishing a corporate business entity for that purpose.

Chapter 3:
Administrative Concerns

To operate effectively and efficiently, your daycare will need many documents including: enrollment applications, vaccination records, liability waivers, payment forms, reservation details, and other basic record-keeping papers. This chapter describes the most common forms required and provides information on how to use them. For sample forms refer to appendix A.

ENROLLMENT APPLICATION
Screening dogs for daycare is vital to the safety of dogs and staff members. Because dogs will be interacting with one another, they must be well socialized, healthy, and current on all vaccinations. The enrollment application starts the screening process to determine whether a dog meets these criteria.

The enrollment application includes several parts: a form with basic owner and dog information, a liability waiver, and documentation from a veterinarian certifying a dog's vaccinations are current. For samples of these forms, see appendix A. Have clients complete the application and return it to the daycare before you meet the dog. Most daycares charge a processing fee that reflects the time spent on the application review. Collect this fee at the time the application is delivered to the daycare. By reviewing this information before meeting the dog, you can often screen out some clients in advance and save yourself valuable time evaluating a dog that is obviously not suitable for a daycare environment.

Owner and Dog Contact Information

Each enrollment application needs to gather basic data regarding the owner and dog names, address, phone numbers (home, work, and cell), and email addresses. Equally important is the information regarding the dog's veterinarian (including phone number and address) and an emergency contact person.

The enrollment application also includes questions regarding the dog's history, previous group play experiences and level of training. This data helps you form an initial impression about the family and identify potential problems you need to discuss with the client before you meet the dog. For instance, if an owner writes on the application that the dog is nervous around large dogs, further questioning can help you determine if your daycare's environment will allow this particular dog to feel safe and comfortable.

CLIENT FILES

Prepare a folder or computerized client file for each dog. This file will contain all forms, notes and pertinent information on a particular dog. This file will be useful for historical data and for future reference when new employees are hired. As you learn more about a particular dog's likes or dislikes, be sure to add these notes to the client file.

Waiver

Have the clients sign a liability waiver before they bring their dogs to daycare. For a sample waiver, see appendix A. The waiver states the clients have read and understand the daycare policies and procedures for enrollment. In the waiver, clients confirm that their dog has been healthy for 10 to 14 days prior to their first day at daycare. They also confirm they have neither seen nor know of any instance in which their dog has been aggressive toward other people or other dogs. Finally, the client agrees to indemnify and hold harmless you

and your staff for problems arising during a normal day of daycare and gives permission for the staff to seek medical attention if warranted. The waiver also includes the clients' obligation to pay any vet bills for medical treatment required for their dog, assuming the injury was not a result of negligence.

Many experts believe a liability waiver may not hold up in court and this may, in fact, prove true. Nevertheless, a liability waiver does keep the clients aware of their obligations and the risks inherent in daycare.

DAYCARE WARRANTY

Some daycares are borrowing an idea from the boarding industry and charging a warranty payment for dogs in their care. This non-refundable warranty is designed to offset and cover any medical charges that may occur in the daycare setting. The client pays the warranty to the daycare.

The daycare warranty can be a standard fee charged each time a client pays for services or it can be charged on an annual basis. For example, most boarding facilities with a warranty charge a nominal fee of $3-$5 per pet each time that pet stays for a visit. This fee is paid up front and covers any expenses which may be required while the dog is in the kennel.

The advantage of a daycare warranty is that a dog in need of medical treatment can be taken to the veterinarian without concern about who will pay the bill. For more information on using a warranty visit the American Boarding Kennel Association website at www.abka.com.

Vaccination Records

Request proof of vaccinations be included with the enrollment application. Routine vaccinations generally include the distemper/parvovirus combination (or DHLPP), rabies, and bordetella. A wide range of veterinary protocols covering these vaccinations exist. Some veterinarians require shots annually; others every three years.

If the daycare is owned and/or operated by a licensed veterinarian, the vaccination requirements may be set in accordance with that veterinarian. However, if the daycare is not owned or operated by a licensed veterinarian, it is best to allow any dogs to attend so long as they are up-to-date on the vaccination protocol their veterinarian uses. Using this same theory, many daycares will also allow titer testing if the dog's regular veterinarian provides proof that the dog is not due for shots.

VACCINATION LETTERS

Track the due dates for vaccinations. A month before the shot is due, send an email to the client with the following note:

Dear Mrs. Jones,

Our records indicate Carrie is due for the following vaccinations next month.
Rabies by 7/5/05
Bordetella by 7/30/05
DHLPP by 7/5/05

Please provide updated vaccination records to our office before the due date to ensure your dog's daycare fun is uninterrupted. You may have your vet fax the records to us at (XXX) XXX-XXXX.

If you have already provided us with updated records, please disregard our friendly reminder. We look forward to seeing you and Carrie very soon.

Thank you,
ABC Daycare

Whether or not the vaccination is required annually or every three years should be up to the dog owners and the veterinarians they use. This will allow you to work within the

protocols of any veterinarians in the area without alienating them. The important thing to track is the vaccination *due date*, as established by the veterinarian, not the date the vaccination was *given*. If the certificate reflects only the date given, the due date for DHLLP will normally be one year, Bordetella will be 6 to 12 months, and rabies 1 to 3 years from the date the vaccine was administered.

Tick and Flea Preventative
If your daycare is in an area prone to fleas and ticks, you may want to require that clients certify they give their dogs a flea and tick preventative medication regularly.

PROCESSING THE APPLICATION
Once the enrollment application has been received, along with the liability waiver, proof of vaccinations and a non-refundable enrollment fee, you will review the documents. Look for potential problems such as any dog that does not get along with other dogs, adult dogs that have never been with many dogs, dogs that show a strong prey drive (like to chase moving objects), or dogs that chase small animals.

Most puppies under five months of age will present little problem to the daycare. However, the older the dog, the greater the potential for problems. Discuss potential problem areas with the client to determine if the dog is a suitable candidate for dog daycare.

If all vaccinations are up-to-date and you feel confident that the dog is a good candidate for daycare, schedule an evaluation of the dog. The evaluation enables you to gain more information about both dog and owner and determine how the dog is likely to respond to other dogs. Often, a dog needs a day or more to adjust to a daycare environment.

Therefore, an evaluation may be more effective at the start the dog's first day of daycare when you will have more time to watch him. For more information on dog introductions, see chapter 7.

**POSSIBLE RED FLAG ITEMS
ON AN ENROLLMENT FORM**

Learn to read between the lines on an enrollment application to help determine if dogs are suitable for daycare. If you think a dog may not be a good daycare candidate, be sure to discuss any issues with the client. You may be able to save yourself time by screening out dogs over the phone if you think they are a high risk in daycare.

- Dogs over 5-6 years of age may find regular daycare too stimulating and may prefer a quieter, senior room, if available
- Dogs over 3 years of age that have never played with other dogs may be overwhelmed and uncomfortable in a daycare setting
- Dogs with noise sensitivities may find daycare too loud and unsettling
- Dogs that guard toys or food from other dogs may fight with other dogs in daycare
- Dogs over 2 years of age that are being brought to daycare to be socialized may be dogs with social issues that the owner is trying to address. These dogs may be candidates for special training but may not be suitable for regular daycare
- Dogs that cannot be handled or try to bite people or other animals may be unsafe for staff handling
- Dogs that like to chase cars, bikes, or other small animals may have a prey drive and may chase small dogs in daycare

---

RESERVATIONS

From the start, encourage clients to make reservations for their dog's attendance at daycare. Taking reservations for dogs attending daycare provides more control for staff scheduling and is important for future planning and budgeting. In addition, by appearing busy, your clients may value your service more.

Some clients will become regulars and will repeatedly attend on the same days (for instance every Monday, Wednesday and Friday or every Tuesday and Thursday). In order to encourage regular attendance - and thereby ensure steady income – give priority reservations to clients who commit to a set routine. Always guarantee these clients a reservation.

SAMPLE
DAILY RESERVATION FORM

Date: Wednesday Aug 3

Paid		Name	Transport	Grooming	Notes
x	1	Denver			
x	2	Carrie		Bath	
	3	Gordo			
	4	Sabre			Lunch
x	5	Missy			
x	6	Max H.		Nails	
x	7	Fifi			Med.
	8	Haley	To home		
	9	Ruckus		Clip	
	10				

For a manual reservation system, track the dogs attending each day, along with pertinent notes for each dog. Software programs are now available for dog daycares. See appendix B for resources.

A simple ledger can track the dogs attending daycare with room to chart additional important information such as special feeding guidelines, medications, grooming needs, transportation requirements, and any special desires of the owner. A low-tech option for reservations is to use a three-ring binder with one sheet per day containing blank spaces corresponding to the number of dogs allowed at the daycare. The binder is divided into 31 days with a corresponding sheet for each date. Each sheet is filled out and changed as dogs are added or subtracted to the particular day. This type of manual system works well and was the mainstream in daycares for many years. However, with the tremendous growth in the daycare industry, a number of good software programs are now available. As your company grows you may find it easier to use a software application developed specifically for dog daycare companies. See appendix B for more information on software.

NO-SHOW POLICY

For most daycares a no-show policy requires a client to cancel a reservation at least 24 hours in advance or be charged the full per day price. This policy allows the staff to plan their days and also prevents overbooking.

PRICING

Determine your pricing policy by analyzing the fees your market can handle and the revenue required to make a profit. For more information on expenses, see chapter 2. You can choose from among several pricing options. Some daycares provide discounts based on the number of days a dog attends each week. Others charge a flat rate per day regardless of the attendance. Billing clients at the end of the month is another option but this policy requires additional paperwork that may become time-consuming as your daycare grows.

Perhaps the simplest pricing method is a payment pass plan similar to those used at health clubs and sporting events. Simply put, a payment pass plan gives a discount depending

on the size of the pass: the larger the pass, the larger the discount per day. Using a payment pass encourages clients to pay a greater amount of money up front in order to receive a per-day discount. This influx of money can ease your cash flow.

A typical scenario for a pass plan might be as follows:
    1-day, $20.00
    5-day pass, $80.00
    10-day pass, $150.00
    20-day pass, $280.00

Maintain the actual pass at the daycare so it is always available when a client needs it. The card is date-stamped each day the dog attends daycare. In order to keep the pass worthwhile, even for infrequent visitors, a pass can be valid for a particular time period, such as 3 to 6 months from date of purchase. For instance, a client who only attends once a week would be able to use a 20-day pass within a six-month period. The more 20-day passes the daycare uses, the more money the business receives up front.

SAMPLE
10-DAY PASS

DOG'S NAME: Cleo   Date Purchased: 6/6/06
OWNER: Mrs. Jones   Date Expires: 12/6/05
                           Cost: $xxx.xx

1_____   6_____
2_____   7_____
3_____   8_____
4_____   9_____
5_____   10_____

For this pass, each line would be date-stamped when the dog attended daycare. When the last line is full, the client would receive a notice to purchase a new pass.

To keep costs down for multiple-dog families, consider a discount for additional dogs in a family. You could base this discount on a percentage of the overall fee, but that may prove to be an accounting nightmare as your daycare grows. If you offer a discount for multiple dog families, keep things simple by charging a set fee for any additional dogs. For example, charge a flat $15.00 per day per additional dog and add this amount to the cost of the pass.

PAYMENT LETTERS

Send the following notice to clients who have used all of their pre-paid days of daycare:

Dear Mrs. Smith,

Just a reminder to let you know today was the last day of your current daycare pass. To ensure your dog's continued happiness at daycare, we invite you to purchase a new pass as soon as possible.

The passes are available for purchase at the customer service window OR you can purchase a pass on-line at www.ourdaycarewebsite.com.

If you have any questions about our services, please let us know. We look forward to seeing you again soon.

Thank you,
ABC Daycare

ACCEPTING PAYMENTS

Initially, most daycares accept only checks and cash, but accepting credit card payments carries significant advantages to your business. First, credit card payments often motivate a client to pay more at once, giving you a stronger cash flow. Credit cards are also easier for clients who do not carry cash or their checkbook. The money is deposited directly into your

account—there is no waiting for checks to clear—so you have more money sooner. Accepting credit cards also saves you time and effort because it eliminates the need to prepare a deposit and take money to the bank.

WHAT ABOUT CREDIT CARD PROCESSING FEES?

Many daycare owners resist the idea of credit card payments due to the service fees charged. If you shop around for a low fee, the service is well worth the extra charge because you will reduce your workload and increase your up-front revenue. See appendix B for merchant service resources.

To establish a credit card option for your daycare, you need to contact a credit card merchant service company. Such companies include Paypal, banks and independent companies. Keep in mind the fees vary widely for these services. Check with your local chamber of commerce for a reputable merchant service company and shop around to ensure you are receiving the most competitive rate.

REFUNDS

If a client does not use an entire advance payment because he moves out of the area, decides to give up his dog, or is asked to withdraw his dog from daycare, you need to have a policy on how to handle the unused monies. Plan in advance how you will handle refunds. You could have a general no-refund policy. However, because daycare is, in fact, a service, this policy is not entirely fair to the client, especially if the daycare staff expels the dog for poor behavior.

A better option is to refund the balance based on actual usage. For instance, if a client purchased a 20-day pass and only used 10 days, charge a 10-day rate and refund the difference off a 20-day pass. Another option, if your business offers additional services or products, is to provide the refund in the form of a credit for such products or services.

CASH CONTROL MEASURES

Always keep money safeguarded. Ensure you have a secure cash register with limited access, a safe with a drop box, receipts with tracking numbers on them, and/or other cash control measures in place. This will ensure your staff is held responsible for all money-handling procedures.

LATE FEES

Charge clients a late fee if they arrive after hours to pick up their dog from daycare. Many daycares charge $1.00 per minute for every minute a dog is left past closing time. If you offer boarding, you might place a dog into boarding and charge an appropriate boarding fee if the client does not pick the dog up in time. However, if you do not offer boarding, you need to arrange for the dog's care until the client arrives: either have a staff member stay with the dog or take the dog to a nearby boarding facility. Either way, the client needs to be responsible for any excess charges incurred as a result of his or her late arrival, and you should spell out your policy regarding late fees well in advance.

LATE FEES AND NO SHOWS

Establish policies regarding cancellations and late pickup charges:
- Sample late fee policy: The ABC Daycare hours of operation are Monday through Friday from 6:30 a.m. to 7:00 p.m. The Center is not an overnight facility. Staff goes off duty at 7:00 p.m. and there is a $1.00 per minute charge for any pet left after 7:00 p.m.
- Sample cancellation policy: Reservations at ABC Daycare are required. Cancellations with less than 24 hours notice will be charged full fees.

REPORT CARDS

Clients want to know how their dog is doing at daycare. Prepare forms that provide information to the clients about their dogs' daily activities. Give such forms to the client anytime the dog's daily activities warrant, for good news or bad. For instance, you might send a note if the dog played on the slide for the first time, played with a new dog, behaved abnormally, refused to eat, had diarrhea, or vomited. Report cards are an excellent tool to enhance your relationship with your client. However, be sure to use these notes for good news and bad, so that your clients do not feel a note from daycare is similar to getting a note from the school principal.

SAMPLE
REPORT CARD

Report card for *Dixie*
Date: *July 7, 2005*

I had a GREAT day at ABC Daycare. I played *in the pool and on the playground equipment* with my friends *Denver, Molly and Sabre* . *Kim and Martha* took very good care of me and wanted you to know *I loved my day, but was too tired to eat lunch.*

The sample above would be pre-printed with blank lines. The sections in italics would be hand written for each dog receiving a report card.

LOGBOOK

In addition to the report card for the clients, notes about the dogs need to be maintained at the daycare. If you see a dog have diarrhea, act lethargic, limp, or exhibit other minor medical concerns, note the problem in a logbook. Then, check the logbook at the end of the day so you can tell the clients about their dogs' behavior.

A computer logbook is ideal, but, at a minimum, the staff can log items of interest in a handwritten notebook kept in the play area. Include the date and time, name of dog and owner, the item of interest, and the initials or name of the person making the entry for each logbook item. It is especially important to note episodes such as dog fights, unusual behavior in a particular dog, and/or dog aggression towards the staff. Include the pertinent information about what was happening before each incident occurred, how they were stopped, and the ultimate outcome in each logbook entry.

SAMPLE
LOGBOOK ENTRIES

June 5, 2004
8:20 a.m. Gotham Smith was very playful today. He slammed into Heidi Jones at 8:15 a.m. Heidi yelped but does not appear to be limping. RK
9:35 a.m. Max Harris vomited. Looks like bile. He is acting normal. CP
9:45 a.m. Max H. vomited again. Pale yellow liquid that looks like bile. He is acting normal. CP
10:15 a.m. Bonnie and Clyde Anderson are growling at one another. Bonnie growls if she is near me and Clyde approaches. I move away and the growling stops. Don't let Bonnie stay near you too long if other dogs are nearby. RK

This routine journaling activity is important. Changes in a dog's behavior can signal the onset of physical problems. Entries in the logbook help you identify trends and prompt more careful observation of dogs that may, in time, need to be expelled from daycare. It also provides the staff with a history of events that occurred while they were not working and allows them to stay up-to-date on the behavior of every dog at daycare.

SERIOUS INCIDENT REPORTS

As with kids on a playground, dogs attending daycare are at risk of injury. Make clients aware of possible minor injuries including: scratches, sprains, bruising, fatigue, sore pads, etc.

Serious injuries to a dog or staff member are also a risk in a daycare. These include superficial punctures, deep scratches, and more serious bite wounds. A serious incident form should be completed and maintained on file at the daycare anytime a dog or staff member is injured. These forms will be important to a veterinarian who treats dog injuries and to injured staff who may need documentation to file worker's compensation claims.

If a bite to a staff member requires medical attention, it may be reported by the hospital to the health department and ultimately, to animal control. Ensure the client is aware of any potential report to animal control so they are not caught off guard if a report is filed.

DAILY AND WEEKLY RESPONSIBILITY SHEETS

Daily and weekly responsibility sheets allow your staff to control their own workflow and free the daycare manager from having to constantly monitor staff activity. In addition, the manager can use the information on the responsibility sheets to ensure one person does not wind up doing everyone else's work. Responsibility sheets list all the activities and cleaning responsibilities needed to be done on either a daily or weekly basis and are used by the daily shift workers as the perform their jobs. For sample responsibility sheets, see appendix A.

CRATE CARDS

If your daycare provides crates for naptime, a 3 by 5 inch crate card for each dog can be helpful. Using crate cards allows you to prepare the nap room in advance. Place the cards on the outside of each crate to identify which dog goes

into which crate. The cards ensure that each dog gets the right food, toys, or other belongings in his crate. The crate cards are also a place to enter routine notes about a dog's naptime needs. For instance, some dogs need a blanket over their crate, and other dogs may be allergic to certain treats.

SAMPLE CRATE CARDS

Max: Do not feed snacks, he has allergies
Cody: Brought her own lunch
Ginger: Cover the crate door to block her view
Missy: Missy and Maggie can be together in a crate

Each entry would be on its own individual crate card and the card placed on the outside of the proper crate.

PLAY AREA CARDS

Play cards are another useful set of easy reference cards. These cards can be maintained in the client file and placed on the wall in the play area at the start of a new day. These cards enable staff to plan and monitor playgroup activity. Play area cards list the dog's name and information regarding playgroup behavior and playgroup suitability. For instance, if two dogs do not generally play well together, their cards would note: "Rover-not good with Max" and "Max-not good with Rover". Having these cards will save time and enable you to visualize the playgroups in advance.

OTHER FORMS

Daycare owners need stationery or post cards for special events (e.g., a new client welcome), get well wishes (for dogs when they get spayed/neutered or have any other surgery), birthday salutations, sympathy cards and holiday greetings cards. It is important you and your staff recognize your clients and their dogs. These kinds of contacts will demonstrate you like the dog and value the clients' patronage.

Provide clients with the excellent service they expect and set your daycare apart from others.

SOFTWARE

In the past few years, several software programs for dog daycares have entered the market. Most programs provide reports to track customer information such as contact data, emergency contact numbers, vaccination due dates, and client reservations and payments. Other possible uses for software include tracking prospective clients and determining how clients heard about you for advertising and marketing analysis. For information on available software programs, see appendix B.

WEBSITES

For customer service, advertising, and cost control a website for your daycares is a must. Daycare owners can significantly decrease their postage fees and administrative time by including all pertinent forms on a good quality website and obtaining email addresses from their clients. At a minimum, the daycare website will include the address and contact information for the daycare as well as all applicable enrollment forms and waivers. This allows clients to either print out the forms themselves (saving you postage and printing costs) or fill out the form on-line for electronic submission. If the daycare accepts credit cards, consider an on-line store so clients can purchase their daycare pass at their convenience. Using emails collected from clients and potential clients, you can send reminders for vaccinations and general information about upcoming daycare activities.

SAMPLE FORMS

See appendix A for copies of the sample forms mentioned in this chapter:
- Enrollment Cover Letter
- Enrollment Application
- Owner Liability Waiver and Health Certification
- Reservation Form
- Payment Pass
- Report Card
- Serious Incident Form
- Office Area Daily Responsibility Sheet
- Office Area Weekly Responsibility Sheet
- Play Area Daily Responsibility Sheet
- Play Area Weekly Responsibility Sheet

Chapter 4:
Facility Layout and Design

The goal of any daycare facility is to provide a safe, fun, and stimulating environment for dogs to play. This chapter discusses how to achieve that goal as you plan the design of your daycare.

KEEPING THE DOGS SAFELY CONTAINED

Safe containment of the dogs is crucial to having a successful daycare. A few items are essential to keep the dogs safe while they are in your facility. These items include: a double-gated area leading to the playroom(s), fencing or walls high enough to confine the dogs, timeout locations to calm down overly exuberant dogs, and distinct areas for separate groups (if you accept dogs of varying sizes, ages and temperaments).

Double Gates

A double-gated containment area is designed to catch any dogs that try to escape through the gate as you open it. For example, in many daycares, the play area is attached to the lobby. If there is only one barrier dividing the lobby from the play area, it is very easy for a dog to slip through this barrier when you open the gate. Such escapes can occur quite quickly and are very dangerous. Loose dogs in the lobby can scare clients and even escape through the front door. To prevent these escapes, daycares need two gates leading into the play area. The second gate acts as a safety barrier. If the dog gets through one gate, he will still be safely confined behind the second gate. The space between the first and second gates need only be big enough to allow room for a

person and dog to move around as they prepare to enter the play area.

PLAY AREA ENTRY /EXIT POINTS

Chapter 2 provides information on types of dogs you may have in your daycare and establishing separate play areas for different groups. When designing your facility layout, be sure to plan the entry and exit path dogs will take to get into each area of your facility. If you cannot safely bring dogs through one area to get to another, you will need to design and install two separate doorways.

Fencing or Walls

Any fencing or wall structures used to contain the dogs must be sturdy enough to withstand the heavy play of large dogs, stable enough to prevent dogs from escaping underneath, and high enough to contain the nimble jumpers. Fencing can be made of a wide variety of materials including chain link, molded plastic, latticework, or drywall. Remember that the dogs will chew whatever you construct. Therefore, wood is not recommended. Wood is easy to chew, more difficult to clean and heavy to move. Appendix B contains resources for fencing and dividers

---

MOVEABLE FENCING

For flexibility in room use, consider moveable fencing structures that can be opened or closed depending on the dogs attending daycare on any particular day. Moveable fencing also allows you to open the room when daycare is not in session to use the facility for other revenue-generating activities, such as seminars, meetings, or training classes.

A high fence is necessary for safe containment of the dogs

The fencing needs to be sturdy and safe. Often, larger breeds such as Labrador Retrievers will slam into the fencing while they play. Smaller dogs may try to slip underneath the fencing. If the fencing is flexible (such as chain link panels), then you will need to add bars to the bottom to prevent a dog from pushing underneath it. If your outdoor flooring is soft enough for dogs to dig in it, you may want to install chicken wire or other low-grade fencing material underneath to prevent an unwanted escape. When installing your fencing, be sure to check the areas between the fence and the walls. Construct the fence as close as possible against the wall to prevent small dogs from squeezing through any gaps.

ESCAPE ARTISTS

Watch for dogs that like to escape. Normally, these dogs will pace the perimeter of a room, looking up and down the barrier as they proceed. If you see a dog that appears to systematically pace the perimeter of the fencing, it may be best to keep that dog on leash until you are sure he will not try to get out of the play area. If he cannot be confined in the play area safely, consider not accepting him in daycare.

Drywall is adequate for the outer perimeter of a daycare play area. However, be prepared to cover holes in the drywall frequently as it is easily broken by the body-slamming play style of some dogs. Tileboard or fiberglass reinforced plastic attached to the wall is an inexpensive way to cover drywall and make the wall sturdier and easier to clean.

NOT ALL CHAIN LINK IS THE SAME

Some dogs have very little body awareness and/or a high threshold of pain. These dogs do not mind running into the fences as they play. If you are using chain link, request galvanized steel rather than aluminum. Galvanized steel is a smoother surface and will not knick, cut, or scratch a dog as easily if the dog rubs against it. Also check to ensure the gauge of wire is suitable for the size of dogs you will be watching.

Make all fencing and walls used to divide and contain groups of dogs at least 6 to 8 feet high. Many dogs can easily jump a 4-foot structure while standing directly in front of the wall. Adding the extra height gives you a buffer of safety.

Timeout Areas

Plan to have a few crates, dog runs, or in-ground hooks (for tethering dogs) if a dog needs a timeout from play. These areas can also be used if a dog is injured and needs to rest. Ensure these timeout areas are easily accessible from different locations within the play area without having to move a dog through the entire room. Plan to have enough timeout areas to accommodate 10 percent of dogs at any one time. For example if you have 30 dogs in a room, plan at least 3 timeout areas. It is important to set up your timeout areas so they are safe for any dog confined to them. Ensure the loose dogs are not able to harass a dog that is taking a rest in a timeout area. Use timeouts for short periods, ideally no more than 5 minutes at a time.

NAP ROOM

In addition to your timeout areas, consider having a separate room for naptime. This room would contain enough crates for each dog, along with feeding bowls and food storage areas. Having a nap room that is separate from the main play area simplifies cleaning the playroom during the day. The separate room also provides you with better control over feeding because the crates can be set up prior to feeding times. Finally, having a separate nap room keeps the crates in better shape. If the crates are located where the dogs can access them easily, they will get chewed on and dogs will urinate on them. Having a separate nap room area will save you money in the long run because the nap room crates will stay serviceable for a longer period of time.

A few crates in the nap room. Note the viewing window too.

PLAYGROUND EQUIPMENT AND TOYS

Dogs at daycare generally play more with one another than with toys. However, like kids, they do enjoy having some fun things to climb and playthings to chew. Avoid using vinyl and latex toys in daycare because these toys can be easily ripped apart and possibly ingested. Hard rubber toys are a better choice.

Special playground equipment, designed especially for dogs, is very durable in a daycare environment and gives your daycare a bright, colorful appearance. Anything the dogs can climb needs to be an appropriate size for the dogs. Small dogs can easily fall or jump off large slides. Even for larger dogs, it is best to avoid play equipment higher than 3 feet. Dog agility equipment, such as tires, tunnels, or jumps, may be used. However, keep all jump heights low to prevent injury to the dogs.

Playground equipment from www.puppyplayground.com

FUN TOYS FOR THE DOGS

Below is a list of fun toys you might consider for your daycare. Appendix B contains a list of vendors for daycare equipment and toys.

Agility Equipment
Indestructible Ball
KONG® Toys
Nylabone® Products
Pit Ball
Puppy Playground Equipment
Rope Toys
Small Plastic Pool
Squiggly Wiggly Ball
Tennis Balls
Tug Toys
Rope Toys

SETTING UP THE LOBBY

Establish a lobby for the daycare where new clients can receive information about the daycare and learn about the facility without disturbing the dogs in daycare. The lobby is the first place your clients see, so make sure it is clean, well-organized, and presents a good first impression. For safety purposes, only allow daycare staff members into the play area with the dogs. However, everyone will want to see the dogs playing. A viewing window, TV monitor, or web-camera will help clients and other visitors see the dog's activities. This compromise allows clients or other onlookers to watch the dogs without getting too close.

OWNER STORAGE

 Provide temporary storage for owners to use at daycare. It is not uncommon for owners to bring in leashes, poop bags, special food, naptime toys or bedding, and various other dog supplies when they bring their dog to daycare. Do not assume that the person who picks up the dog knows everything that was brought in with the dog. Provide nametags on bins, hooks, or cubbies so there is no confusion. When I first opened, I often had clients pick up the wrong leashes and go home with their dog. This in frustrating for both the clients and your staff. Once I started using nametags, this frustration was eliminated.

Make the lobby large enough to allow several dogs and clients to enter without the dogs bumping into things. Do not clutter the lobby with anything that can be easily knocked over by the strong tail of an exuberant dog or pushed over by a dog that might jump up on it. Avoid anything that will be ruined if a dog urinates on it; this will happen fairly often. Set up the lobby so that clients can easily write checks or fill out paperwork with their dog safely tethered, freeing the client's hands to write. Set up a reception window so you can interact with the client from a separate room. It is best if your administrative office area and supplies are separated from the lobby. This will provide better protection to your office from dogs that may not always be under the control of their owners, and also keeps all your client information out of view of customers and other visitors.

Adding flags to the ceilings can help decorate the room

ADMINISTRATIVE OFFICE

You and your staff will need an administrative office within which to conduct all business matters. Ideally this office will be connected to the lobby so you can deal with clients who come into the facility with their dog. Your office will contain all the forms, client files, notebooks and other office supplies needed for the daycare. Chapter 3 deals extensively with

administrative matters and will help you understand how to organize your office space.

DECORATIONS

Your daycare needs to be decorated in a way that makes the facility look like a fun place to stay. Here are some inexpensive ideas for decorations:

- Bright paint on the walls
- Large garden flags hanging on the walls or from the ceilings
- Acoustic tile covered in fabric and attached to the walls or ceilings (also helps deaden noise)
- Sponge painting with cutout paw pad sponges
- Vinyl stickers or wall paper cutouts on the walls
- Murals or other painted pictures
- Enlarged photos of client dogs
- A bulletin board of client dogs
- Framed posters or drawings
- Simple curtains made of dog-themed fabric
- Safe, non-toxic plants that hang from ceilings

A mural is a nice way to decorate the walls of a facility

OTHER AREAS

As you plan the layout of your building, remember to include space for other uses such as grooming, boarding, and training if you will offer those services. Keep in mind that it takes most daycares two years to generate a consistent profit. Offering other services, or renting out your facility to other companies, may generate some additional income.

INDOOR FLOORING

Your indoor flooring surface must be easy to clean, non-slip, and cushioned for the safety and comfort of both staff and dogs. There are a wide variety of good flooring surfaces that range from the relatively inexpensive tile to the more expensive liquid rubber. Ultimately, you will base you flooring decisions on your budget, the size of the floor, and your planned uses of the facility. Appendix B contains resources for flooring companies.

Tile

Commercial tile is perhaps the cheapest type of flooring. Tile is very easily mopped and disinfected but can be slippery for the dogs and the staff. If your space is relatively small (under 2000 square feet of play area), then tile may be a feasible option because the dogs do not have a large space to run and the potential for injury is reduced. The use of tile in a facility larger than 2000 square feet is not recommended because the danger of a dog injuring himself while running increases in a larger tile-floored facility Tile is also not a good choice if you plan on conducting any dog sports classes, such as agility, in your building. When installing tile, make sure the seams are tightly fitted to prevent the possibility of urine, water, or other liquid seeping into and under the tiles.

Epoxy Sealed Concrete

If you have concrete floors, using an epoxy sealant mixed with sand is an option. This type of floor is painted on in layers. First, a heavy duty sealant is placed on the floor. Once it dries, colored epoxy paint is placed over the sealant and then sand is broadcast into the paint to add traction. Epoxy sealed concrete is a reasonably priced alternative for cement floors. This non-skid floor is colorful and easy to clean.

Rubber Mats

Rubber mats provide much better traction than tile but may be a little bit more difficult to clean. As with tile, the seams need to be closed with a sealant to prevent leakage. Rubber mats come in a variety of sizes and shapes and range from rolls of rubber that can be unrolled on the floor to small square pieces that snap together. Horse-stall mats, normally 100 lbs per mat and sized at approximately 4'X6', are commonly used in daycares and provide excellent cushion for both daycare activities and most dog sports.

EDPM

One of the newest products being used in daycares is Ethylene Propylene Diene Monomer (EDPM) rubber. This product is normally used as a roofing material, though many daycares are now using it on the floor. It is sold in large rolls of varying thicknesses. Some daycares opt for the thinner, less-expensive rubber and install padding underneath. You need to ensure the EDPM floor is installed properly, with no bubbles, and will need to seal the seams as well.

Liquid Rubber Floors

Liquid rubber floors provide good traction and comfort for dogs. These floors are poured on the floor and covered with a protective sealant. Because it is liquid rubber that hardens on the floor, these floors are seamless with no chance of liquid getting under the floor. The liquid rubber floors can include a cove base that also prevents liquid from getting under the

walls. However, these floors can be difficult to clean if the surface is textured. You may need a scrubbing machine or kennel brushes, rather than a mop, to clean the floor completely.

DRAINAGE

When considering your indoor and outdoor flooring, take note of the pitch or slope of your floors. If water or urine is spilled on the floor, where will it flow? You will need to know where water will run off if you spray the floors with water or a cleaning liquid to clean them. Outdoors you need to know where the water will run off if you hose down the play area. If you have no natural slope, you may need to build one into the floor when you add the flooring materials.

OUTDOOR FLOORING

Outdoor areas can consist of grass, asphalt, gravel, dirt or mulch. Each has its own advantages and disadvantages, and most daycares use more than one type. In general, whatever is used outside needs to be replaced periodically.

Grass

Grass is easily destroyed and turns into mud. It is also difficult to clean and disinfect. If you start out with grass, plan on replacing it every few months or rotate the dogs' play areas to allow grass to grow in one area while dogs play in another.

Asphalt

Asphalt is a good surface, but provides no cushion for the dogs. It is sanitary and quite easy to clean. If your outdoor area is relatively small, asphalt is a nice choice. However, asphalt does get quite hot in summer sun so shade will be necessary if your daycare is in a sunny location.

Gravel

Gravel, such as river rock or smooth pea gravel, is commonly used in daycares. Placing the stones on a dirt or sand base

will help provide drainage. Gravel is relatively easy to clean and disinfect. However, dogs often get sore feet when they first use the gravel surface. Chapter 8 contains information on pad injuries.

DO I NEED AN OUTDOOR AREA?

Ideally, a daycare will include both indoor and outdoor play areas. This allows the dogs to have bathroom breaks outside, in a more natural environment. However, my first daycare was all indoors. If dogs are kept indoors only, then you may want to walk the dogs on a rotating schedule so they are provided with a chance to go to the bathroom outside. Some indoor facilities that do not provide daily walks have potty stations made of grass or mulch, but the success rate of these potty stations varies considerably. See the section on bathroom breaks in this chapter for additional information.

Dirt and Mulch

Both dirt and mulch can be used in an outdoor location but both tend to get the dogs dirty and are hard to keep smelling fresh. Disinfecting dirt and mulch is not easy and the material needs to be replaced frequently. Dirt and mulch is most commonly used as a base surface underneath other surfaces.

BATHROOM AREAS

Nothing draws more questions from the daycare clients than the subject of dog bathrooms. "Where do the dogs go to the bathroom?" is one of the most common questions you will hear from prospective clients. In reality, the dogs will go to the bathroom wherever they want, but that is not the answer a client wants to hear.

Clients are most comfortable if they know you have set up a specific area for use as a dog bathroom. This might be an outdoor grassy spot or a small indoor area with dog litter.

(Interestingly, few clients ask, "Does my dog use the bathroom area?" They just want to know that one exists).

DOG BEHAVIOR AND YOUR FLOORING

When preparing your indoor and outdoor surfaces, keep in mind that dogs often eat anything near them. This includes mulch, rocks, and sometimes even grass. Many dogs like to dig, so dirt and mulch floors may become a large digging pit for some dogs. Supervision is required to ensure the dogs do not ingest materials that can be harmful to them or escape from the play yard.

A small potty area with mulch contained within PVC pipe

TAKING DOGS TO THE BATHROOM

Generally, every dog will go to the bathroom within 5 minutes of entering the daycare despite the client's claim that, "He just went outside." So always give each dog a bathroom break in your designated area as soon as he arrives.

Dogs can learn to go to the bathroom in a designated location at daycare, and this can help to reduce the amount of area the staff must spot clean. However, do not think you will eradicate accidents in all other areas of the daycare. You will clean urine and feces on a continual basis regardless of your dog bathroom arrangement.

HOUSETRAINING AND THE DAYCARE ENVIRONMENT

Dog owners are often concerned that if their dog has a housetraining accident in the daycare, they will also have accidents at home. This is a myth. Dogs are very good at learning they can do one behavior in one location and another behavior in a different location. If a dog is housetrained in his home, he will remain housetrained at home - even if he has occasional accidents in daycare. Remind your clients that their homes do not have 30 canine residents with all their attendant odors. Their dog will definitely know the difference between home and daycare!

NOISE CONTROL

When setting up your daycare, look for ways to deadening sound in your play areas. If you are in a warehouse with high ceilings, any barking will reverberate in the room. Certain types of wall structures, such as aluminum or cement, will increase this reverberation. Although the dogs may not bark constantly, they will still bark enough to cause considerable reverberation – and literally headaches – for your staff. The noise may also be stressful to the dogs. Appendix B contains ideas on noise-deadening materials and resources on hearing conservation.

WEB CAMERAS

More and more daycares are providing web camera services. With a web camera, daycare footage is shot through a small camera mounted in the play area. This footage is then uploaded to the daycare website where clients can view their dogs playing anytime throughout the day.

Web cameras can enhance your marketing plan because many clients will show the website footage to other friends, co-workers, and family members. Visitors to your website get a first-hand look at how much fun the dogs have at daycare. In addition, clients enjoy tuning in to see their dogs having fun during the day.

PROVIDING WATER FOR THE DOGS

Make water available to the dogs at all times while they are playing. Place the water bowls in a low-traffic area to limit dog play and puddles. If you have dogs that love water, consider hooking water buckets with handles to the walls to prevent tipping. Another great alternative to bowls are drip-type water bottles that dogs easily learn to drink from but cannot tip over.

Chapter 5:
Personnel Matters

One of the most challenging points in your business will come when you have to hire your first employee. Unless you have a trusted friend or client who is looking for a job, you will probably be looking for a new hire from your community. Good workers are a goldmine so take your time when hiring and find someone who is willing to work hard and be a part of your dream.

JOB DESCRIPTIONS
Each employee needs a clear understanding of his or her job. This will help the staff work together as a team without stepping on each other's toes. It will also allow you to pay wages in accordance with the responsibilities expected of each person. Appendix A contains suggested job descriptions.

HIRING AND FIRING
There are many ways to find new employees. First of all, people may walk in off the street and ask if you have any job openings. Even if you are not looking for employees at that particular time, ask them to fill out a job application. Keep these applications on file for future reference. When you have an opening, always go through your on-file applications first. Some of the people will have found jobs, but others may still be available for an interview.

Another way to find employees is to check with people you already know. Ask your local veterinarians, groomers and boarding facilities if they have any recommendations for

reliable employees. Other pet-related companies sometimes have animal-loving employees who want additional work. Also, ask your clients for referrals because sometimes a client's family member may be looking for a job.

EMPLOYMENT ADVERTISEMENTS FOR FREE

Here is an idea from Bob Payne of Molly's Country Kennels in Lansdale, PA: Some banks and other merchants publish newsletters that accept employment ads from their clients. For Molly's Country Kennels, a major source of part-time employees has been from the local bank's newsletter job ads, which cost nothing.

If you have to advertise in the classified section of your local newspaper, be prepared to spend several hours doing interviews over the phone or in person. Your ad will draw a wide variety of respondents and you will need to screen them carefully.

AVOIDING DISCRIMINATION

Remember that hiring/firing processes must be non-discriminatory. One good way to support your hiring decisions is to use a standard list of questions for each applicant interviewed and use a scoring system to match them to your job description requirements. This will allow you to make decisions based on the skills of the potential applicant and the needs of your business and helps to avoid discrimination.

It takes several weeks to properly train a new employee, and the last thing you want is a person who quits after you have invested time training them. Be sure new employees understand the volume of work involved in a daycare. Many potential employees will tell you they want to work at a daycare because, "I love dogs and want to play with them all

day." These employees soon realize there is very little play and quite a bit of hard work involved at a daycare. Your employment application needs to make clear what is involved in working at a daycare. See appendix A for an example of an employment application disclaimer.

It may be beneficial to start a new employee out at a lower wage for a probationary period of 1 to 3 months. This gives both of you time to adjust to the new job, new work schedule and new personalities. You can decide if the new person will fit into your business, and the employee can make a decision about the new job. If there is a good fit, then the employee will receive a raise after the probationary period.

A WORKING INTERVIEW

Consider an idea I received from Dawn Walton at The Dog Zone in Cedar Rapids, Iowa. After completion of an initial interview, potential employees are scheduled for a 3 hour, paid *working interview* in which the prospect works in the daycare group with a manager or assistant manager. This allows the manager to evaluate the applicant's reaction around rowdy dogs and their understanding of dog behavior and body language. It also gives the applicant a chance to experience the work environment of a daycare. This working interview helps screen potential new employees in a more realistic manner.

Once you hire your employee, provide written feedback on employee performance at regular intervals. A copy of such feedback will be provided to the employee and the original placed in the employee's personnel file. At least once a year, provide each employee with a written performance review. This is a formal way of acknowledging the employee's strengths and weaknesses. However, providing informal feedback throughout the year is also important.

If an employee is not performing up to your standards, you will need to document any problem areas and show what counseling you provided to help the employee improve. Put your conversations in writing and have the form signed by the employee as well as by the manager conducting the counseling. If matters do not improve, you will have the unfortunate task of firing the employee.

Firing is never easy, but is sometimes necessary in any business venture. Documentation showing trends in poor performance can help to safeguard your business from any legal action a former employee may try to bring against you. Documentation will also support your business if an employee files for state unemployment payments. These charges can increase the tax payments for your business. See appendix B for a list of helpful human resource information.

ACCENTUATE THE POSITIVES

Too many people focus only on the negative aspects of an employee. Do not ignore the positives. The common phrase, "Praise in public, criticize in private" bears repeating. Always make a special effort to acknowledge your staff when they do good things, regardless of how small. Employee recognition is important to the morale of your staff and will help employees remain loyal to your company. Remember to tell your staff when they have done a good job, bring them lunch from time to time, offer to take them out for a meal or provide them with a gift certificate to a local nail salon or retail store. Rewards do not have to be expensive, but they do need to be sincere.

EMPLOYEE COMPENSATION

Determine employee compensation based on the skills and responsibilities of the staff members. Match each job description to a range of pay based on the job responsibilities. Use your job descriptions to make sure the employees who are responsible for more get paid more. Nothing causes more

contention among staff members than unfair compensation policies. Do not think the staff will not talk about how much they make...they will. You need to ensure your pay scale is fair based on the employee skills and responsibilities assigned.

How much you pay your staff depends on your location, expenses, and business plan. When discussing compensation with the staff be sure to quantify the non-monetary benefits such as vacations, sick days, and insurance benefits. See box titled Benefits for Employees.

LABOR LAWS

For-profit businesses do not usually qualify for volunteer labor. It is very important that you understand and follow federal labor and fair compensation laws. This is one area where consulting with an accountant may be necessary. Violation of payroll tax remittances can cause severe penalties from the Internal Revenue Service.

EMPLOYEE MANUAL

Put together an employee manual for your staff. An employee manual helps set the stage for a professional operation. Your staff will learn up-front that you take your business seriously and operate it professionally. The employee manual will inform employees of the history, philosophy and employment practices of your company and also explain what is expected of the employee. In addition, an employee manual describes the benefits you will provide to your valuable employees.

An employee manual will include some of the following basic information: personnel administration and organization, policies on hiring and firing, non-compete agreements (if you use them), standards of conduct, dress codes, information on compensation and performance, benefits, leaves of absence for holidays, vacations or sick days, and basic staff responsibilities.

See appendix B for recommendations on software to help build your employee manual. Be sure to have your lawyer review any legal policies and procedures in your employee manual to ensure they are in accordance with state and federal laws.

BENEFITS FOR EMPLOYEES

In most cases, your staff will not be highly paid. Therefore, it is important to reward them with non-monetary incentives. Often, employees stay at a company more for the way the company makes them feel than because of the pay. Here are some suggestions for benefits you might provide your hard-working staff. Those benefits marked with an asterisk are required by law in most states, others are freebies you offer.

- Annual party or outing
- Continuing education in animal behavior classes
- Discounts on merchandise sold at your facility
- Free daycare, training or grooming
- Free (or subsidized) vaccinations for pets
- Health insurance benefits
- Paid holidays
- Paid vacations
- Personal leave of absences
- Sick leave
- ABKA employee training and certification programs
- Attendance at trade shows, educational seminars, industry meetings
- *Unemployment compensation insurance
- *Worker's compensation insurance

DOG HANDLING POLICIES AND PROCEDURES

In addition to your employee manual, which will cover administration of your staff, you will want a dog handling policies and procedures manual, which will cover the physical work aspects of your staff's jobs. This manual will

contain the policies and procedures governing your daycare such as how interact with the dogs and how to handle undesirable behaviors of dogs in daycare. This policy manual will help keep you and your staff safe as they deal with the dogs.

DAILY SCHEDULE

The daily schedule you establish at your daycare will dictate your staff schedule. Because daycares cater to working families, most daycares open early and close late. A normal day at most daycares runs from 6:30 or 7:00 a.m. until 6:00 or 7:00 p.m. This makes for a long day and will require your staff to work in shifts.

There are numerous ways to plan a day at your daycare. Some daycares schedule particular games, training sessions or nap periods at pre-determined times throughout the day. Other daycares use a basic routine without scheduled activity times. To allow for smaller staffing, some daycares rotate groups of dogs between playing and kenneling. Other daycares provide special massage, grooming and/or training sessions for each dog in daycare. Keep in mind any individual attention you give a dog may require additional staff members.

I recommend, at a minimum, you schedule a naptime for the dogs. Not only will this provide the dogs with a well-needed break - it will also allow your staff to relax. A naptime usually consists of crating or tethering all the dogs to prevent them from playing and allow them to settle down and sleep. You will find dogs have peaks and valleys during the day; you will have periods of times when the dogs rest on their own as a group. However, left to their own devices, the dogs will not take the same amount of rest as they would if you put them in crates and turned off the lights. Ideally, naptime will take place in a separate room set up for this purpose.

When you develop a naptime routine, consider the stress level and temperament of each dog. Most dogs do fine in a crate once they get used to it. Some dogs prefer a closed crate while others do better in an open crate. Some dogs settle down more quickly if the crate or crate door is covered with a blanket. To help tethered dogs sleep, erect visual barriers to keep them from seeing and trying to reach the other dogs. Any naptime routine will include monitoring each dog for stress and adjusting the routine as needed for that particular dog. Chapter 6 contains more information on understanding and handling stress in dogs.

A CASE FOR NAPTIME

When I first opened my daycare I did not offer naptime. However, each day from approximately 11:00 a.m.-12:00 p.m. and again from approximately 3:30 p.m.-4:30 p.m. the dogs would all lie down and sleep. Therefore, I thought a naptime was unnecessary. The dogs were doing fine on their own.

Cindy Briggs, owner of All Dog Playskool in Richmond, Virginia, convinced me to try naptime. It was one of the best decisions I ever made. Once the dogs had become adjusted to the naptime, they were easier to manage in the afternoon. I never thought the dogs were grumpy in the afternoons. However once I compared their new afternoon behavior with their behavior before we instituted a naptime, it was obvious to me the naptime did, indeed, help them sleep more soundly and wake up better rested for their afternoon activities. In addition, my staff was better rested after two hours of office work and human interaction without constantly monitoring the dogs.

SCHEDULING THE STAFF

Schedule your staff members in the most efficient and economical manner possible. Remember that payroll in a well-run daycare accounts for a very high percentage of overall expenses, and you will need to be prudent in

scheduling. Staff on duty during slow periods can take lunch breaks, assist with routine cleaning chores, and perform administrative duties. Consider using the naptime period to have employees email photos to clients, put up bulletin boards, enter new client data into computers, update logbook entries, prepare mailings, contact veterinarians about shot records, etc. Keep a list of to-do items which can prevent your staff from doing nothing during naptime. If there is not enough work to keep the staff occupied during slow times, do not schedule them to work.

EMPLOYEE SCHEDULING

Here is a suggested daily schedule for a small daycare (up to 25 dogs) that opens at 6:30 a.m., closes at 7:00 p.m., and offers a naptime from 11:30 a.m.-2:00 p.m.

6:15 a.m.-3:15 p.m. Opening shift for full-time employee (includes a one-hour unpaid lunch break during naptime)

6:15 a.m.-11:15 a.m. Opening shift for a part-time employee

10:00 a.m.-7:00 p.m. Closing shift for a full-time employee (includes a one-hour unpaid lunch break during naptime)

2:00 p.m.-7:00 p.m. Closing shift for a part-time employee

Note that the part-time employees work before and after the naptime period. During naptime there are fewer staff members on duty.

STAFF TO DOG RATIOS

"How many employees do I need?" This is a common question. Generally, for the safe monitoring of the dogs you will want to staff your daycare at a ratio of one employee to every 10 to 15 dogs, depending on the size of the dogs and the experience of the staff. However, even if you start with less than 10 dogs, as soon as possible hire at least one more

employee for safety reasons. If you are alone, it will be difficult to handle any rare emergency situations that may arise.

For a new employee, monitoring a small group of 10 dogs will be a challenge. Do not put new staff members in that position without supervision. Even for an experienced staff member, watching more than 15 dogs can be risky. If a fight breaks out, it will be difficult to manage a room of 15 dogs with just one person.

When scheduling the staff, keep in mind that those assigned to the daycare have the primary job of watching dogs. If you must also meet clients, make phone calls or handle administrative maters at the same time, you will need an additional staff member on hand. It is quite difficult to manage the group of dogs and try to focus on a client or administrative matters simultaneously.

STAFF TRAINING

To keep the dogs and the people safe the staff must be constantly aware of dog interactions. Close supervision will prevent most problems. For this reason, at least one employee must always be physically located anywhere dogs are playing. The only way to intervene quickly enough to prevent problems is to be in the same room as the dogs. The goal is to intercept any potential problem behavior before the behavior escalates. By getting to know the dogs and learning how they play, you will be able to identify which dogs to watch more closely than others.

It is important to train your staff properly. The staff must understand dog behavior, body language and canine social interactions. Dog handling policies must be taught to all employees as well. Staff members need to understand how to deal with unwanted behaviors such as jumping (on people) or barking. Most daycares use some deterrents for undesirable behavior, and staff members need to know the safe and effective way of using these methods. Chapters 6 and 7

provide more detailed information on controlling a group of dogs in a daycare setting. Color-coding dogs' collars based on behavior can help new employees identify dogs with particular concerns until staff members learn all the dog's names.

AVOID THIS MISTAKE

When I began hiring staff members, they received on-the-job training. Usually this meant I would place them with a group of dogs that had always done well in daycare. Inevitably, this normally well-behaved group of dogs would have scuffles and squabbles while being supervised by the new employee. This occurred several times before I realized what was happening.

The dogs always got along well as a group because an experienced staff member was supervising them. When a new employee, who did not know what to watch for or when to intervene, began to watch that same group of dogs, the dogs had problems. It is comparable to a substitute teacher having problems in classroom. I learned that the level of appropriate behavior in a daycare playroom depends greatly on how well the staff member is doing his or her job. Early intervention is the best prevention for fights. Members of your staff must be trained properly before they can be left alone to supervise a group of dogs, even if those dogs have always played nicely in the past.

The primary job of the staff is to monitor the dogs and prevent fights from occurring. This responsibility cannot be overstated. The effectiveness of your staff can make the difference between a daycare that has problems with aggression and fights and one that does not. Your clients have entrusted the care of their very special dogs to you. Therefore, you have a duty to keep those dogs safe from any harm during their stay at your daycare. Ensure all the policies and procedures you have for dog handling are clearly taught to your staff and ensure the staff is supervised in the first few

weeks of employment. Start them off with small dogs and be sure to teach them the subtle nuances of the dogs in your care.

CUSTOMER SERVICE

Good customer service can bring in more long-term clients than anything else you do. Always strive for excellent customer service and consistent enforcement of policies. A good goal to achieve is the WOW factor. That means doing anything you can to make your clients leave your office saying, "WOW! That was great." Anytime you can achieve the WOW factor, you will get closer to having a long-term relationship with that client and, in all likelihood, gaining numerous word-of-mouth referrals as well. Your staff needs to offer this same high standard of customer service.

Clients love their dogs, and you need to love them too. At the very least, you need to be able to convince your client you love their dog, even if it is not entirely true. One of the primary reasons given by clients who leave a daycare is simply, "I didn't think they liked my dog." Causal comments such as, "Well, he's crazy, but that's because he's a Lab" can sometimes be taken offensively by a Lab-loving owner. Do not think just because you also own that particular breed means it is okay to make negative comments about them. Clients often take these statements very personally. Teach your staff to put a positive spin on anything they need to tell the clients.

You and your staff are dealing with a client's baby, and you need to give them absolute assurance their dog is in excellent care. Keep clients aware of their dog's behavior during daycare. Be honest if their dog is involved in an incident or accident while in daycare. Report cards, web photos and daily debriefs to the clients are all ways to keep them informed and build their trust. Use logbooks and good verbal communication between shifts so all information is shared among employees as well. Clients will ask about their dog's day at daycare and you never want an employee to say, "I

don't know. I just got here." Comments like those turn customers off and makes them feel as if you do not care about their dog. See chapter 3 for more information on administrative matters in the daycare.

GETTING YOUR CLIENTS TO SAY, "WOW"

Use some of these ideas to really wow your clients by providing excellent customer service that will keep them coming back!

- Teach your employees to learn each dog's name AND each client's name. Greet all humans and dogs with their name.
- Make a photo collage of their dog's firsts: first day at daycare, first day on the slide, first day in the pool, etc.
- Send a hand-written thank you card to any client who sends you a referral
- Send a hand-written thank you to all clients for choosing your daycare
- Send a birthday card greeting to dogs on their birthdays or adoption days
- Send get well cards to dogs that are sick or recently had surgery
- Host bachelor and bachelorette parties before puppies are neutered/spayed
- If a family has a new baby, send them a card from their dog
- Send photos to clients via email during the day
- Put photos of a client's dog on your website
- Pick a dog of the month and write a story about him for a monthly newsletter

Plan Your Phone Calls Carefully

Staff members need to be able to provide good service on the phone as well as in person. If you have a staff member with poor customer service skills, keep that person off the phone. Those who do answer the phone must know all the services your daycare provides and the answers to any questions prospective clients may ask. Do not answer the phone if you are rushed or too busy to give your prospective clients the attention they need. Train your staff using a telephone flowchart and prepare them for the wide variety of questions they will be asked. Let them practice phone techniques with you or another staff member acting as the customer. See appendix A for a sample telephone flowchart.

The most important goal of any phone call is get a prospective client into your facility. Keep phone calls brief and use them to set up a time for a prospective client to come to your office, ideally with all forms in hand.

Do not rely on a phone call to persuade the prospective client to enroll his or her dog in your daycare. Such persuasion is more effective when the person is standing in your lobby, not while the person is talking on the phone. An exception to this principle may occur when the caller has been referred to you by a veterinarian or friend. Often, such referrals are sold on your services even before they call.

Do not spend too much time on the phone. Be polite and provide some basic information, then quickly refer the individual to your website where they can download the pertinent information they will need to bring in to your office.

Suggest the prospective client fill out the paperwork and recommend a tour of your facility to the caller. Ideally, you will provide the client with an exact date and time of the tour. Get an email address and follow up with a brief email reminding the prospective client of the tour time/date and include a link to your office website and the forms they need. Then, call or email the client one day before their

appointment to remind him or her of the meeting. This will help to reduce the number of individuals who do not show up for an appointment.

Handling Client Problems

Nothing is more difficult for clients to hear than negative news about their pet. Keep in mind that people need acceptance and they fear rejection. So, when you have something bad to tell a client, you need to be sensitive to an individual's feelings and tread lightly. Often, it is best to give them some advance warning, then tell them, then follow up with a phone call or another meeting after they have had time to process what you told them.

EXPELLING A DOG FROM DAYCARE

One of the hardest things to tell a dog owner is that their dog is no longer welcome in daycare. Some dogs are just not suitable for the daycare environment. Some puppies mature and no longer play well as adults. Some dogs just are not happy being with other dogs.

When talking to the client, try to remember that your message is painful for the clients to hear. Most clients feel they have a bad dog if the dog cannot attend daycare. Help the client understand that their dog is wonderful and that the daycare environment is the problem, not the dog. If possible, provide alternatives for the dog and client, such as a pet sitter or day boarding facility.

Always be sure to follow up with the client the next day in case they have additional questions about their dog's behavior. In many cases, you will end up repeating many of the same things you told the client initially. This is to be expected because it is hard for clients to process negative information about their dog.

Keep your clients up-to-date on the behavior of their dog. A client whose dog has to be expelled from daycare should never be surprised by this news. Clients need to be informed if their dog is not doing well or is having particular issues.

They also need to be told how you are trying to handle their dog's issues. Let the client offer some suggestions to help you resolve any problems with their dog. Continue to keep them updated so they are not surprised if their dog eventually needs to be expelled.

Do not be misled by the client who hears bad news and takes it well. Always follow up with a phone call the next day. You will often find after some time to process the information, the client is either incredibly understanding or incredibly angry. The best way to respond to such anger is with empathy and concern. Often, working through these feelings with the client can help them realize that what you are doing or saying is in their dog's best interest.

Chapter 6:
Understanding Canine Behavior

This chapter deals with one of the most important issues for a daycare owner – supervising a group of dogs interacting off-leash. Understanding the behavior of dogs is vital to operating a safe and successful daycare. Failure to understand such behavior is dangerous in a daycare environment because oversights can result in injuries to both people and dogs. Your staff must learn to intervene before problems occur.

Early intervention is possible only if you can predict behavior of dogs when they are playing. This skill results only when you truly understand canine social group dynamics. Appendix B contains a list of resources for additional information on understanding canine behavior. The information in this chapter will better prepare you to use the dog handling policy information contained in chapter 7.

CANINE BODY LANGUAGE

Understanding how dogs look when they are *submissive* or *dominant* is not enough. By the time the dogs have reached the stage where they are showing examples of *dominance* or *submission* often seen in books on body language, the dogs are too far into the behavior to respond easily to human intervention. Your staff needs to identify and understand all the subtle changes in dogs that lead to these dramatic examples of behavior. This chapter will help you to understand some of the important keys to keeping the dogs in your daycare safe.

SEPARATING DOGS

Dogs attending daycare must be placed in suitable playgroups based on the sizes, ages, and temperaments of the dogs in you care.

No matter how well large dogs and small dogs play together, you have a risk of problems when you put the two groups together. Large, adolescent dogs often do not have the coordination to avoid stepping on a smaller dog, especially if the larger dogs begin to run. However, larger older dogs may prefer the smaller, calmer dogs to the rambunctious younger dogs of their own size. The canine prey drive affects the interactions of some big and little dogs. Dogs with a strong prey drive will instinctively chase and nip at smaller, active dogs. In a daycare setting this type of behavior can quickly get out of control and result in an injury or death. (See the box entitled Predatory Drift later in this chapter.)

In general, older, calmer dogs can be placed with small, calm dogs, but the larger, rowdy, and adolescent dogs need to be in a separate group. Depending on the sizes of these groups, staff members may want to divide them further to make the groups more manageable.

Puppies under 5 months of age need their own space until they are large enough to play with the bigger dogs. Daycare provides wonderful socialization for puppies but overwhelming a puppy in a group of large dogs can be detrimental to the social development of the puppy.

DESIRABLE AND UNDESIRABLE BEHAVIOR IN DAYCARE

Certain behaviors indicate desirable play among dogs in a daycare while others are more problematic. Throughout the course of each day, your staff will observe a continuum of behavior. You need to teach your staff to differentiate between desirable and undesirable behavior in the daycare environment.

DESIRABLE AND UNDESIRABLE BEHAVIORS FOR DAYCARE

Desirable:
- Play Bows
- Lateral Movements
- Repetitive, Exaggerate Movements
- Low, Slow, Tail Wag
- Relaxed, Fluid Body

Undesirable
- Bullying Another Dog
- Playing Too Rough
- Mounting
- Too Much Arousal

Play Bows

Play bows are desirable. A play bow is a stance in which a dog is holding his chest and head to the ground with his front paws straight out while his hindquarters are in the air. It is a classic signal that one dog would like to play with another. Not all dogs will accept the bow and play, but it is a good sign if one dog is offering it to another.

Lateral Movements

Side-to-side, lateral movements from dogs indicate a dog is playing, not trying to stir up trouble. Playful dogs will often jump side to side or spin while playing.

Repetitive, Exaggerated Movements

Repeated motions, especially when they are exaggerated movements, are wonderful. You will often see dogs leap wildly into the air or repeat the same spinning motion when they are playing. These exaggerated movements use up more energy than the dog would use if he were actually going to fight.

This dog is doing a play bow

Low, Slow, Wagging Tail

A low-hanging, slow, relaxed tail wag is usually a friendly sign. A relaxed tail carriage—neither tightly wrapped over the dog's body nor tucked underneath—is best. If this is coupled with a slow, steady, rhythmic wag, that is even better.

Bullying Behavior

A dog that is picking on another dog in an intense manner needs to be redirected for the safety of the group. Do not allow dogs to bully one another. Remember that each dog needs to be having fun. If one dog is having fun and the other dog has his tail constantly tucked, the dogs need to be separated. You do not want the bully to practice his bullying behavior at the expense of another dog. Such behavior helps neither animal.

Dogs Playing Too Rough

A dog playing too roughly with another dog is a problem in daycare. This is often a result of mismatched play styles and can be resolved by putting the rougher dogs in a different group. If two dogs are playing roughly and both enjoying it, then the behavior is not a problem. However, if one dog is rough and the other dog is trying to hide, neither dog is benefiting.

WHEN DO I INTERVENE OR REDIRECT BEHAVIOR?

Generally speaking it is best to interrupt the dogs playing fairly often. The longer dogs play uninterrupted, the more difficult it becomes to change their focus. In general, if you think the playing seems serious, then stop the game before it escalates. Do not wait until the dogs are in a full-blown fight before you attempt to intervene. It is much better to be proactive than reactive in a daycare environment. For more information on how to handle inappropriate behaviors, see chapter 7.

Mounting

Dogs will sometimes mount one another during daycare. This is generally a sign of assertiveness by one dog over another. Most dogs will stop this behavior on their own. However, it is a potential area of tension between dogs, especially if the mounting dog is persistent. If the mounting behavior continues, it is best to intervene and redirect the dogs.

Each dog should be put in a group where proper play is encouraged and undesirable behavior is prevented. This will keep the dogs happy and the staff safe.

AROUSAL AND AGGRESSION

The term *arousal* when used in conjunction with dog behavior is meant to describe a state of high energy. This can be positive energy, which might occur when a dog is very excited about playing, or it can be negative energy in which a dog is overly stressed. In a state of high arousal, most dogs will display signs such as dilated pupils; high-pitched, repetitive barking; and/or hyper, nervous behavior such as pacing or jumping excessively.

The more activity in the room, the higher the arousal level will be. **Arousal levels and aggression in dogs are very closely linked.** One can easily lead into the other.

Arousal and aggression in dogs are very closely linked. Highly aroused dogs are likely to become aggressive

Therefore, the goal of the daycare staff is to keep the arousal level down. When watching the dogs play, be wary of any dog that seems to be overly stimulated. Sometimes it is easy to confuse the state of high arousal with a highly social dog that just wants to play. A highly aroused dog will usually have dilated pupils, excessive panting, half-moon eyes, and will be more frenetic and stiff than a social dog that is not aroused. Allow the dogs to interact, but do not let them play uninterrupted for long periods of time. Regardless of how well the dogs are playing, watch for signs that the dogs are becoming overly stimulated and aroused. Intervene early and often to prevent the arousal levels from becoming too high.

PLAY STYLES

Keep similar play styles together. Like kids, dogs have their own unique ways of playing. These styles can be categorized into four basic groups with some variations within each group: chasing, neck biting, cat-like and body-slamming. Some play styles work well together and others do not.

JUST LIKE KIDS

The daycare dynamic is very similar to the behavior of kids on a playground. What may start out as two kids taking turns pushing one another (full of giggles and laughter), suddenly becomes a shoving match with angry cries of "You hurt me!" and "You are not my friend anymore." This sequence is also predictable in dogs. If you allow their state of arousal to continue for too long, over-stimulation can cause the dogs to begin to fight.

Chasing

This play style involves dogs that like to chase other dogs as well as dogs that enjoy being chased. The game sometimes begins with one dog playfully stalking another. Ideally, you will have at least one dog that chases and one dog that likes to be chased so they can have fun. If you end up with two dogs that both want to chase, but neither wants to be chased, the chasing game never gets underway. Chasing in the daycare environment can sometimes cause over-excitement in the other dogs in the room. Therefore, limit the game to only one or two minutes at a time.

In addition, watch for dogs that shift into predatory behavior during the chase. A dog that is having fun chasing is relaxed and loose. The dog that becomes predatory looks stiff, fixated, and intense. This behavior, sometimes called, predatory drift, can easily get out of hand and become aggressive if it is allowed to continue.

Remember that the chasing or stalking games require a dog willing to be chased. If one dog is chasing another and the dog being chased is showing signs of fear (e.g., tail tucked, showing avoidance, trying to end the game), then that dog is not having fun. Such chasing borders on bullying, obnoxious behavior and needs to be redirected.

PREDATORY DRIFT

Daycare staff members need to understand the concept of predatory drift when working with dogs. This is the behavior that occurs when a dog's instincts take over his behavior due to something in the environment. In other words, what starts out as play, *drifts into* something predatory. Predatory drift can occur during chasing games, when the quick motion of a dog fleeing can trigger the chasing dog to attack more aggressively. Predatory drift can also occur when a dog begins making a high-pitched yelping sound. This sound can sometimes trigger other dogs to drift into prey mode to attack the noise-making animal. Predatory drift can be deadly in a daycare and is more likely to occur between small and large sized dogs.

A few dogs enjoy a game of chase

Neck Biting

The neck biting play style is often seen when the dogs are too tired to get off the floor. Instead, the dogs lie on their sides, head to head, and mouth each other's neck and face. In this type of play, the dogs are loose and relaxed. If a fight were actually going to occur, the dogs would need to stand up first. This is a fairly benign play style. Interestingly, this is the play style many clients find most alarming. When the dogs are grabbing each other's necks, they do show their teeth and they make contact with one another's hair and skin. Many clients become concerned that this type of play injures one or both dogs. Educate the clients and your staff on the style of play and point out the relaxed body postures and calm behavior of the dogs in play.

These two dogs are engaging in neck biting style of play. Though the dogs are showing teeth, their bodies are relaxed and loose

The neck biting play style is more aggressive if one dog stands over or appears to pin the other dog on the floor. Again, this may start out as play. However, if the dog doing the pinning does not allow the other dog to get up, a scuffle could erupt. Intervene if a dog has another dog pinned on the ground, even if they appear to be playing.

Cat-like

The cat-like play of some of the smaller dogs includes gently batting one another with front paws. Cat-like play can also include quick, exaggerated motions in which dogs spin around one another without touching each other.

FAIR AND BALANCED PLAYING

The best playing occurs when dogs are fair and balanced in their play. Ideally, the dogs will take turns being on top of one another. They will alternate pinning one another on the ground or jumping on top of one another. Fair and balanced playing is generally relaxed and fluid. Dogs engaging in this sort of play will take breaks from time to time. The dogs will calm themselves down by stopping the play on their own and then resume the play after a momentary pause. This is the best sort of play among dogs in a daycare.

Body-Slamming

The body-slamming play style is the primary wrestling play of the larger, sporting breeds which generally involves dogs knocking into one another, coupled with wrestling on the floor. This play style can be quite rough as dogs slam into one another (as well as the walls of your facility). The body-slamming play style needs to be monitored so the dogs do not become overly stimulated. The body-slammers usually do not work well in a group of dogs that prefer the cat-like play style. The body-slamming types will have great fun smashing into the smaller breeds. However, little Fifi, the Poodle, will not appreciate the antics of Ruckus, the Labrador, if they are put together. Despite their high threshold of pain, the body-slamming dogs can hurt themselves if they are allowed to get too rough with one another. Intervene and slow them down from time to time to prevent their play from becoming uncontrollable.

STRESS SIGNALS

There are some key behaviors evident when dogs begin to get uncomfortable. These behaviors, often called stress signals,

are important in identifying dogs that need intervention from the daycare staff. The dog may need a break from the play or perhaps just a new playmate. Sometimes dogs will show signs of stress when they first arrive in daycare and need time to settle into their new routine. Dogs can become stressed by over-stimulation as well. In general, if you begin to see a dog with many stress signals, it is time to intervene. Any dog that is under stress is more likely to show aggression. The staff must be able to identify these signals quickly and use them as early signs for intervention.

Yawning
Yawing is easy to identify in dogs. Often, dog owners mistake a big yawn for a tired or content dog. In reality, yawning is thought to be a sign that the dog is releasing some tension. He is a little nervous and is trying to calm himself or another dog by yawning. Yawing usually indicates a dog is not interested in playing.

Scratching/Sniffing/Stretching
Does the dog show interest in something and then suddenly begin scratching, sniffing or stretching? These are all ways in which dogs relieve their stress or deflect attention and frustration. Obviously dogs scratch, sniff, and stretch for other reasons as well. However, when any of these behaviors occur continuously in the same cycle, they are probably related to stress. For example, an client tells their dog to sit and the dog suddenly feels the urge to scratch his neck.

Lip Licking
Like yawning, lip licking is a sign that a dog is tense or nervous. Lip licking is very easy to see, but goes unnoticed by most dog owners. Pay attention not only to the fact that the dog is licking his lips, but how quickly it happens. Generally speaking, the more stress the dog is experiencing, the faster the lip licking. Dogs licking their lips often have tight muzzles, another sign of tension.

Lip licking is a common sign of stress in dogs

Shaking Off

Shaking off is a common behavior after a dog has had a bath or gone for a swim. It is also a behavior dogs will do when they are dry and are releasing tension. You will often see this behavior when two dogs meet. They may separate from one another and then shake off as if to say, "Whew, that was stressful." Some dogs may do this after playing for a few minutes in order to give themselves a break.

Panting

All dogs pant to cool off. However, when panting is excessive for the amount of exercise the dog has done, it is often a sign of stress. If a dog enters the room for his first day of daycare and he is panting immediately, this is probably a sign of nervous energy and has nothing to do with exercise. Tightening of the muzzle while panting is also an indication of stress.

This dog has not been exercising. However, she's panting pretty hard. Notice the tightness in the muzzle. You can see veins popping out at the back of the mouth. Her ears are also back.

STRESS IN THE CRATE

If you are using crates for the dogs, be sure to watch for some of these stress signals when crating and uncrating a dog. Some dogs will freeze or their pupils may dilate just prior to being crated. This may make them more difficult and unsafe to handle. Other dogs may enter the crate but continuously drool once inside. If a dog is unable to handle being in a crate, then use another method of confinement for that dog.

Dilated Pupils

Dilated pupils are sometimes difficult to notice in dogs. However, highly aroused dogs will often have very dilated pupils. The greater the arousal in a dog the more likely he is to show aggression. Dilated pupils are an indicator that a dog is stressed and may need some time to settle down.

The dilated pupils can be seen in this dog.
The ears are also back and you can see veins
or muscles popping out on the face

Drooling

Dogs under stress may sometimes drool. This is often seen in the more introverted dogs that otherwise appear calm and quiet. Sometimes the only thing you will notice is excessive long, stringy drool coming from the sides of the dog's mouth. In the absence of food, this is usually a sign of stress.

LISTEN TO THE SOUNDS

Teach your staff to listen to the various tones of each dog. Barking, growling and whining can all occur in a wide range of pitches for each dog. You will soon learn to identify a single dog's bark from an entire group of dogs. You will also learn to identify sounds that mean a dog is playing and those that mean a dog is injured or scared.

Half-Moon Eyes

Half-moon eyes refer to the look of a dog's eyes when they are wide-opened, and you can see a portion of the whites of

the eyes on the outside of the eyeball. Usually, when a dog is relaxed, you seldom see the whites of their eyes. Be wary when half-moon eyes are combined with a stiff body posture because this combination is often a precursor to aggression.

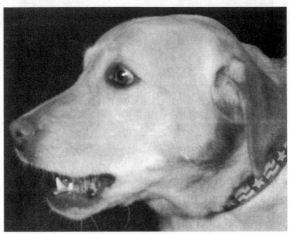

Half-moon eye

IS IT STRESSFUL OR NORMAL?

Many dogs will show one or more stress signals throughout their day at daycare. The stress signals are meant to be guides for your staff. They provide early indicators that better prepare the staff to prevent problems in daycare. However, a dog that is showing one sign is not necessarily overwhelmed. The key is to observe and understand how many stress signals a dog is showing. If there are many signals, then try to reduce the source of stress for the dog. Also, as you get to know the dogs in your care, you will be able to identify what is normal behavior and what is more extreme for each particular dog.

Avoiding Eye Contact
When dogs avert their gaze from a person or other dog, they are sending a signal that says they want to be left alone. They are asking for some space. When they do, respect their request and give them time and space to relax. Some dogs,

will rebound right away; other dogs need more time. Often eye contact avoidance is accompanied by the dog lowering his head and turning away slightly.

This dog shows avoidance by turning away.
You can also see one half-moon eye

Clawing/Jumping

Some dogs will claw and jump at people and/or other dogs when they are nervous. At first glance, this appears to be inappropriate behavior from an untrained dog. However, in a stressed dog this behavior takes on a more panic-stricken feel. These dogs are looking for help and need relief from whatever is causing them stress.

Piloerection

Piloerection is a fancy name for what happens when a dog's hair on his back comes up. Most people assume raised hackles are a sign of aggression. However, this is not true. Piloerection is a sign of general arousal and not necessarily a sign of aggression. Dogs that display piloerection are usually becoming over-stimulated through play, or they may be nervous or scared. Either way, is best to intervene to give them time to settle down.

TAILS AND EARS

Teach your staff to watch the subtle movements of a dog's tails and ears. You can understand quite a bit about the dog's emotional state by looking at these two body parts. Tails tucked far under the body indicate nervousness or fear. Stiffened tails carried high indicate arousal. Ears can fluctuate from a relaxed state to ears flattened back in fear or defensiveness. Watch these body postures to help you understand when to intervene. In the photo the black dog is approaching with tail high, but ears are slightly back. The white dog is clearly nervous with a low, tucked tail and ears flattened in nervous apprehension.

WARNING SIGNALS

Stress signals are your first clue that a dog requires some time to calm down. Warning signals, often occurring in conjunction with stress signals, are generally immediate precursors to a fight. Your staff needs to be able to differentiate between stress and warning signals. Warning signals are a little more serious and require immediate intervention.

Stiffness

Dogs that are stiff are usually tense and stressed. Their rigidity may be seen in a stiff legged stance or tightly flexed hindquarters. You can also see tension in the face and muzzle of dogs. Usually this tension will appear in the form of veins or muscles tightening on the face or a furrowed brow.

Freezing

Freezing can begin as a subtle sign, but is one that becomes stronger the more stressed the dog becomes. Initially, watch for quick behaviors that might alternate between a relaxed stance and stiffening. However, if the freeze becomes longer in duration, redirect the dogs. Dogs usually freeze when they enter a state of arousal that begins to border on fight or flight.

PUTTING IT ALL TOGETHER

This chapter discusses many individual stress signals and warning signs as a means of helping you understand canine body language. Keep in mind that you will never read one individual sign without the context of the rest of the dog's behavior. As you learn to identify the individual signals you will need to learn to put them all together to obtain the best understanding of the dog. This is a skill that takes time to develop. Practice daily by watching dogs as much as possible. This will best allow you to predict future behavior in the daycare dogs and keep yourself and the dogs safe.

Direct Stare

Watch for a dog that seems intently focused on another dog or engages in excessive, aggressive stalking. If the dog's stare is frozen and stiff, especially if the rest of the body is stiff, intervene to distract the dog. Even if the other dog looks away, intervene to break the eye contact of the staring dog's eyes.

Head And Chin Over Another Dog's Shoulders

Dogs often posture over one another in an attempt to assert control. One sign of this assertiveness is a dog that puts his chin and head over another dog's shoulders and back. Such behavior does not indicate a fight is about to begin but nevertheless is a clear sign that one dog is beginning to assert himself over another. If the display is quick, there is no need for concern. However, if the display continues and the

movements of one dog over the other dog become more forceful, then intervention becomes necessary.

SHOULD I LET THE DOGS WORK IT OUT?

As a trainer, I do sometimes advise family pet clients to let dogs work out their issues on their own. However, I do not recommend such non-intervention in a daycare setting. Allowing the dogs to work it out may result in a fight involving the whole group of dogs, not just the ones that are trying to work things out. In addition, an incorrect assumption that the dogs will work things out without actually fighting may result in an injury to a dog that does not belong to you. You are there to keep the dogs safe and to intervene rather than letting dogs work out their own issues.

Pinning a Dog

If one dog pins another to the ground and then freezes on top of him, intervene immediately. This behavior will often cause the bottom dog to panic, and a fight will ensue as the lower dog attempts to get up. While dogs are playing, they may pin one another, but they should relinquish control once the pinning happens. In an ideal situation, there is a balance to the play and the dogs will switch position, taking turns pinning each other down rather than one dog always pinning the same dog.

Pushing a Dog to the Point of Submission

Anytime a dog continues to push himself on another dog, even after the dog shows signs of avoidance, you need to intervene. If a dog is being chased and then ends up becoming overwhelmed and hiding, the chasing dog needs to be redirected. If two dogs are playing and one nips the other, causing a yelp, both dogs should stop playing on their own. If they do not stop, you need to intervene to help the two dogs play nicely or place them in separate playgroups.

Lifting Lip in a Snarl

Far too often, humans ignore the tiny muzzle movements associated with a lip snarl. Ideally, dogs will use as little force as possible to end an unpleasant encounter. This means, ideally, dogs will lift their lip in a snarl before they growl or snap. If this happens, it is important that your staff identify the behavior and intervene immediately. Do not make the dog increase his aggressive posture because you did not heed the snarl. Lip-curling movements in the dog's muzzles can be very small. Observe all of them and intervene regardless of the size of snarl. It is a clear signal that the dog is uncomfortable.

POSTURING: IS IT NORMAL OR NOT?

As you begin to observe dogs more closely, you will find there are wide variations in these warning signals. How do you know if the signal is normal posturing behavior, which will end, or if it is a precursor to a fight that should be redirected? Generally speaking, if the behavior changes relatively quickly and the dogs become relaxed and playful again, then the behavior is normal playing. Continue to monitor the play. However, if the behavior intensifies, intervene.

A good clue to the intensity of the dog's behavior is to watch both the dog giving the signal and the dog receiving the signal. If a dog is displaying some warning signal and the other dog backs away, the behavior will probably end on its own. On the other hand, if the receiver becomes more challenging, the interaction could become more serious. With experience you will begin to see subtle, but dramatic differences in the dogs and you will understand when intervention is most important

---

Growling

Dogs will sometimes growl in play. These playful growls are accompanied by loose, relaxed body postures, low tail carriage and desirable behaviors and movements. When growling is accompanied by a direct stare, freezing or

stiffening, or if it is deep and low, the behavior needs to be addressed immediately. Redirect the dog, or dogs, growling and reduce their tension. There are times when one dog will growl and another dog will begin to bark at him. This can cause the growling dog to retaliate with aggression directed at the barking dog, even if the original growl was directed at a different dog. Growling tells you the dog is reaching the end of his rope. He needs your help.

RESOURCE GUARDING

Dogs sometimes guard the things they find valuable. Experts call this practice resource guarding. As a daycare owner you need to understand and be able to identify resource guarding behaviors because fights between dogs for control of resources can become very violent.

The important thing to understand about resource guarding is that the value of an item is very subjective. Not all dogs will guard the same items. Resources can include obvious items such as food or treats, but can also extend to other valuable commodities: water, toys, favorite sleeping spots, and people. I have even seen dogs guard things people consider disgusting, such as dog poop and vomit.

Because we cannot always identify exactly what a particular dog will consider valuable, the staff needs to be able to identify the signs of resource guarding.

Many of the warning signs mentioned earlier apply to resource guarding behaviors. The signs are coupled with obvious attachments to a space, person, toy, or food. If the item is in the dog's possession, he will normally hover over it, circle it or stand near or on it. If you notice dogs leaning against or circling you, often growling at other dogs that come close, this is a sign that the dog is guarding you. If a dog is lying on a bed and growls when other dogs approach, the dog is guarding his bed. Watch for early signs such as freezing, lip licking, and curling the lip because those signs

will almost always precede the more obvious signals of growling, lunging, and barking.

In most cases, removing the resource will resolve the problem. If the dog is guarding a person, the person needs to walk away from the dog; if the dog is guarding a bed, the bed can be removed from the room. Chapter 7 contains additional information about staff policies for resource guarding issues.

DOGS WHO DO NOT SPEAK DOG
Occasionally you will find a dog that does not seem to understand canine body language. They will ignore blatant warning and threat displays from other dogs. Often, these are dogs that have been taken from their litters early, they were raised as a singleton pups, or they were just not exposed to positive play experiences as young dogs. A common scenario looks something like this:

Remington, the little 7-month-old clueless puppy, is playing with Sierra, the adult German Shepherd Dog. Sierra is resting and prefers not to be bothered by Remington, so she shows her teeth when Remington approaches. Remington, not recognizing this overt signal, continues to bounce around Sierra offering play bows and barking. Sierra then growls to show Remington she means business. At this point, Remington, still ignoring the warning signs, pounces on Sierra's head. Sierra aggressively nips him on the ear.

This is a fairly common encounter among some dogs. If a dog owner is watching this scenario, the owner will normally reprimand Sierra. Most owners are embarrassed by any displays of aggression, and Sierra seemed very mean. In reality, Remington should have been redirected. Sierra told him, in very obvious dog terms, that she wanted to be alone. Remington ignored the rules of canine language and continued to be a pest. It is unfair to punish Sierra in this instance because she did what dogs do...she increased her aggression because the lower level was not working.

DO NOT PUNISH THE GROWL

Human beings are hard wired to discipline undesirable behavior. It is in our nature. If you understand signals leading toward aggression are on a continuum from subtle signs, such as freezing, lip licking, and growling to more obvious signs, such as lunging and biting, you will understand why it is important not to punish dogs when they show aggression.

Ideally, I want dogs to use as little force as possible when they decide to display signs of aggression. If a dog curls his lip at me or growls and I back away, I have taught the dog that low levels of aggression work. Do I want to teach a dog that aggression works? Not necessarily...but in that instant, when I am getting the lip curl or the growl, I have reached a critical point in which I am no longer in training mode. I will move away to avoid a situation in which the dog's aggression must escalate. I can use my experience as an indicator of future training protocols later.

However, if I punish that lip curl or the growl, I have done nothing except teach the dog that low levels of aggression do not work. This may cause the dog to escalate to higher levels of aggression immediately in the next similar situation. This is how you can end up with dogs that seem to bite without warning. That is definitely not what I want in daycare because I rely on my staff's skills of observation to keep the dogs safe.

Reading the dogs is the key to the staff's success, so do not punish the dogs for providing you with information you need to read. If a dog is growling in a daycare environment recommend the client contact a trainer through the Association of Pet Dog Trainers (www.apdt.com) for help.

In the scenario above, we hope that Sierra inhibited her bite so the nip did not do physical damage to Remington. In a daycare environment you will not necessarily know a dog's level of bite inhibition. Therefore, pay attention to the dogs that do not seem to understand canine language. They need assistance. Redirect them from a dog that is telling them to

stay away. More information on bite inhibition is located at the end of this chapter.

FIGHTING

Normal playing includes a great deal of play-biting and wrestling between the dogs. However, these games can sometimes escalate into more serious scraps if you and your staff do not monitor the dogs closely. By getting to know the dogs and learning how they play, you will be able to identify which dogs to watch more closely than others.

In general, if you think the playing seems serious, then stop the game before it escalates. Do not wait until the dogs are in a full-blown fight before you attempt to intervene. Most squabbles can be broken up by distracting the dogs and redirecting their behavior. However, waiting until a fight occurs will require much more work to stop. Chapter 7 contains staff policy information on breaking up a fight.

If a fight occurs in a daycare, crate every dog in the room, not just the dogs fighting. During a fight a group mentality sets in and can cause other dogs to join the fray.

GROUP MENTALITY

One problem with a fight in a daycare setting is the group mentality that occurs when a fight breaks out. There is great agitation among all dogs when fighting occurs and the dogs on the periphery of the fight will often begin nipping and snapping at the fighting dogs. These dogs need to be controlled just as much as the fighting dogs. Train your staff to react immediately if a fight happens. In addition to crating the fighting dogs, tether or crate all dogs in the room. Be wary of the smaller, shyer dogs. In the heat of the action, they will often find the courage to begin fighting as well. The group mentality that erupts when a fight breaks out is very

dangerous and is one of the main reasons for proactive staff supervision and early intervention. Always have an employee in the room with any loose dogs. The ideal ratio is 1 person for every 10 to 15 dogs.

REDIRECTED AGGRESSION

Be careful in any instance in which a dog is showing aggression. Though his aggression may be directed at another dog or person, dogs can become frustrated and redirect their aggression onto any animal or person that is nearby. The new victim could be you, a staff member, or another daycare dog.

BITE INHIBITION

A dog's level of bite inhibition is a big part of the decision on whether or not to remove the dog from daycare. Any altercation in which a dog causes a serious puncture to another dog need to be reviewed. These injuries are usually considered grounds for the removal of a dog from a daycare. A dog that leaves a deep puncture on another dog has little bite inhibition and is not a safe dog to have in daycare. Dogs use their mouths all day long during play. They have an amazing ability to control the level of bite if they have learned to do so. On the other hand, a dog that intends to inflict injury can do so with amazing speed. Dogs that lack bite inhibition are not good daycare dogs. The chart below is a guide to evaluating a dog's bite inhibition. Chapter 5 provides information on expelling dogs from daycare.

	DR. IAN DUNBAR'S BITE LEVEL ASSESSMENT *(printed with permission)*
#1	Obnoxious or aggressive behavior, but no skin-contact by teeth.
#2	Skin-contact by teeth, but no skin-puncture. However there may be nicks (less than 1/10" deep) and slight bleeding caused by forward or lateral movement of teeth against skin, but no vertical punctures.
#3	One to four punctures from a single bite with no puncture deeper than half the length of the dog's canine teeth. May be lacerations in a single direction, caused by victim pulling hand away, owner pulling dog away, or gravity (little dog jumps, bites, and drops to floor)
#4	One to four punctures from a single bite with at least one puncture deeper than half the length of the dog's canine teeth. May also have deep bruising around the wound (dog held on for *x* seconds and bore down) or lacerations in both directions (dog held on and shook its head from side to side).
#5	Multiple-bite incident with at least two Level 4 bites.
#6	Flesh consumed or victim dead.

In general, there is a huge transition between appropriate versus inappropriate use of the mouth when you cross into Level 3 and above. Dogs in daycare that display inappropriate bite inhibition (level 3 and above) need training and should not be in a daycare setting.

Chapter 7:
Dog Handling Policies

STAFF RESPONSIBILITY

Your clients have entrusted the care of their very special dogs to you. For that reason, your top priority must be to keep those dogs safe while they stay at your daycare facility. Your staff will determine whether you can consistently honor that priority. Proper training of your employees and written dog handling policies are important aspects of a safe daycare environment.

> As a staff member, you are not so much
> every dog's friend , as you are a hall monitor
> to make sure the place is safe.
> ~Kathy Minnick, The Animals' House, Sterling, VA

PLAY AREA ACTIVITY LEVEL

Remember: the greater the activity in the play area, the greater the potential for a fight. For this reason, discourage horseplay and exuberant activity by your staff. Such activity will only heighten the dogs' overall state of arousal and increase the potential for problems. The staff's job is to monitor the dogs' activity, but not create unruly play between the dogs. Staff interaction with the dogs needs to be calm and controlled.

PICKING UP DOGS

Teach staff members to refrain from picking dogs up while they are in the daycare play area. It is tempting to pick up and

cuddle the small dogs and very easy to pick them up to move them. However, this activity will often cause other dogs to jump in the air and nip at either the staff member or the dog being held. If small dogs need to be moved through an area where large dogs are playing, put the small dog in a crate for safety. If a small dogs needs to be protected from a larger dog, block the dogs' view of one another by physically moving in between them, rather than by picking up the smaller dog. Alternatively, use a leash to move the larger dog away from the smaller dog.

THE BLOODY TAIL

One of the bloodiest accidents I have seen in a daycare involved a tail wound caused when a staff member picked up a small dog. The small dog was picked up to be moved into another area. While the small dog was being held, a larger dog jumped up and grabbed the tail of the smaller dog causing several lacerations down the side of the tail of the smaller dog.

The small dog was panic-stricken, the employee was distraught, and the floor was covered with blood. Thankfully, the small dog recovered, but this type of accident can easily be avoided by prohibiting the staff members from picking up the dogs.

HANDLING AND MOVING DOGS

Dogs need to be moved or otherwise handled while they are at daycare. You will often need to move dogs away from the gate in order to get another dog through. You might have to move a dog into a crate. You may have to handle a dog to take off or put on a collar. However, no matter why you are handling the dog, you and your staff need to be careful when doing so.

Grabbing a dog's collar rapidly is a bad idea. A dog may be startled or even snap if suddenly grabbed by the collar. Instead, use a slip-lead that can be put over the dog's head

and around the neck to move the dog. Keep a slip-lead readily available at all times.

Also, avoid pushing dogs into each other while moving them. Just like people, dogs have varying spatial needs. Some dogs require more space around them than others. Pushing one dog against a dog that requires more space may result in a dog fight.

IDENTIFYING DOGS THAT NEED EXTRA ATTENTION

If grabbing a dog by the collar or neck results in the dog whipping his head around toward your hand, the dog needs an evaluation by an experienced staff member. This behavior, even if it does not result in injury to your hand, can escalate into snapping or biting. Unless you have the staff and time available for private one-on-one training, daycare is not the place to work on desensitization of this behavior. However, you do want to prevent your staff from making the behavior worse.

Use extra care when moving these dogs. Using a leash looped over the dog's head or clipping a leash onto their collar (if the dog does not react) instead of grabbing the collar will keep you safe and prevent the dog from practicing undesirable behavior that could escalate into greater aggression. Remember: practice makes perfect, but this is not a behavior we want the dog to strengthen. Identify these dogs with a brightly colored collar as a visual reminder to the staff.

CROWDING

The potential for a dog fight increases when the dogs crowd around people or into a tight space. Avoid any behavior that might encourage crowding of the dogs. Dogs may crowd you if you are talking to or petting one of them. They may also crowd you if you sit or stand against a wall or piece of play equipment. If dogs begin to crowd around you, move away from the dogs and do not provide any attention to them.

Crowding will also occur at the gates when dogs first arrive and when they go home for the evening. It is best to limit the number of dogs that have access to the gate where dogs are arriving/departing to reduce the crowd and decrease the potential for a fight. Dogs that are overly stimulated at the gate and otherwise difficult to control when other dogs are arriving or departing should be removed from the daycare area during busy times.

SITTING IN THE PLAY AREA

Arrange seating areas for your staff that keep the staff off the floors and away from walls and corners. Placing yourself lower than the dogs will generally cause the dogs to crowd around you in order to gain your attention. This can cause injury to you if the dogs jump on you and injury to the dogs if they begin fighting each other to gain your attention.

Place chairs used by the employees away from walls or corners so dogs that are close to staff members will not feel trapped or cornered by the other dogs. This will also help to make dogs attempting to seek attention from the employee less likely to crowd another dog and trigger a fight.

FOOD/FEEDING

The best way to prevent fights over food is to prohibit food in the daycare play area. This includes employee food as well at treats for the dog. Food may be used to encourage a dog to sit prior to going home. However, such food use needs to be done when a dog is alone and away from the other dogs. Even then, monitor the dogs in the daycare area for potential resource guarding behaviors. See chapter 6 for more information about resource guarding.

Feed dogs separately, ideally in their crates. If a dog does not like the crate, feed him in a separate room, an empty section of the play area or in a dog run where he can safely eat without other dogs nearby. All food must be completely cleaned up before letting dogs back into the play area. Teach

staff members not to reach into a crate to remove a bowl until the dog has left the crate. This will help to prevent any resource guarding behaviors and possible aggression toward the staff.

THE USE OF FOOD IN DAYCARE

I discourage the use of food in daycare because it can trigger resource guarding behaviors. However, some daycares have had great success using food to help with training and reinforcement. If you want to use food for these purposes, use the following guidelines:

- Test all dogs for resource guarding with other dogs. Keep in mind resource guarding towards people and dogs are two different behaviors. The presence of one type of resource guarding does not necessarily mean the presence of the other. Therefore, dogs must be tested with people and with other dogs.
- Test dogs with more than one dog. Because food may be provided to the group as a whole, conduct resource guarding tests with at least 5 to 6 dogs in an open space which will be more indicative of the manner in which the food will be used in a daycare setting.
- Use treats that are of very low value such as kibble. Generally speaking, the more valuable the resource, the more likely the dog will guard it.
- The staff needs to have excellent observation skills and be able to identify early warning signs of resource guarding in order to prevent potential fights. For more information on observing warning signals in dogs, see chapter 6.
- Any dog that is a resource guarder with other dogs should be prohibited from attending a daycare that uses food in group settings.

CRATING/UNCRATING

Dogs are crated from time to time in order to rest, have a timeout, and take a nap. If the dogs are wearing collars, remove them when the dogs are crated for naptime. This policy will prevent a dog from getting tangled and possibly injuring himself while in the crate.

Keep in mind naptime crates may contain food. Once he is in the crate the dog will begin to eat and may have a stronger potential to guard his food. To minimize any resource guarding, do not reach into a crate while a dog is eating.

To remove a dog from the crate, simply open the door and allow the dog to come out of his own free will. If collars are being used, slip the collar back on the dog as he exits the crate or as soon as he comes out. If, for some reason, the dog does not come out of the crate, *do not reach into the crate to move him!* Even without food in the crate, a dog may feel cornered and may bite. If time allows, simply wait for the dog to exit the crate on his own accord. If you cannot wait for the dog to exit on his own – and if no other dogs are around – you can attempt to lure the dog out with a food treat. If this tactic is also unsuccessful, tip the crate forward to encourage the dog to come out.

Fleece blankets help many dogs relax in the crate. Some dogs are also more comfortable with a covering over the front of the crate. Experiment to see what makes a particular dog most relaxed. Annotate these comments on the dog's crate card for future reference. See chapter 3 for more information on crate cards. Classical music played during naptime will help the dogs calm down and sleep. If a dog is unduly stressed in the crate (excessive drooling, barking, whining, howling) then allow that dog to sleep in a more open space such as the main play area or the office.

ENTRY/EXIT TIMES

Dogs crowd doorways and sometimes fight over space when other dogs come into or leave the daycare. Some dogs get agitated when excitement erupts in the daycare (such as during the arrival and departure of other dogs). Manage this problem by limiting access to the main entryways during busy times. Crate or leash any excitable dogs during busy times. Dogs that like more space will often become aggressive when they are crowded at the gates. These dogs might be happier if they are crated during the arrival/departure periods so they can avoid the stressful crowded situations. Be mindful of those dogs that do not like being moved by their collar during these periods of high activity and keep a leash on them if they need to be moved. Refrain from grabbing dogs by their collars if you need to move them; use a slip-lead instead.

WHAT TO EXPECT WHEN DOGS MEET

New dogs' behavior will range from *scared to death* to *ready to play immediately*. Even dogs that have played in other dog parks or daycares may need time to adjust to new surroundings. It is perfectly normal for new dogs to be slow to initiate play. If they prefer to hide for a period of time, allow them to do so – but do not let the other dogs harass them. Often, the new dog just needs time to relax and will come out to play on his own terms once he is feeling a bit more confident.

Be wary of the dogs that have no fear and come in ready to play. These dogs are often seen as the playful pet, perfect for daycare. In reality, these dogs are often over-stimulated and highly aroused. They are more likely to stumble into a fight than the more cautious dog that is taking the time to size up his new friends.

NEW DOG INTRODUCTIONS

There are several different methods for introducing a new dog to your daycare group. Each method has its own advantages and disadvantages. You will need to evaluate your own staff's strengths and weakness to determine which method is best for your daycare. Regardless of the method used, introduce a new dog slowly and carefully. Start by allowing the new dog to get accustomed to a small group of non-reactive dogs. Add more dogs as the new dog becomes more relaxed. A poorly managed introduction can ruin a dog's first experience in daycare and prevent him from adjusting well.

Some daycares set up specific days and times to introduce new dogs to the daycare environment. This is advisable because you can make sure you have extra staff members on hand to assist. I always did introductions in the early morning on a regular day of daycare. The new dog was scheduled to show up during the first two hours of daycare. This provided us with more time to evaluate the dog on the first day because he would stay with us after the introduction.

USING SPECIFIC DOGS

It is not uncommon for a daycare owner to use their own dog for all new dog greetings. I do not encourage this policy. Meeting new dogs on a continual basis is stressful even for the most happy-go-lucky, social dogs. It can burn them out eventually. I prefer to use daycare dogs already attending daycare for my new dog introductions. Because I am using whatever dogs are attending on a particular day, there is wide variation in who is the *first dog* to do the greeting. It is never the same dog over and over again. If you always use the same dog, especially if it is your own dog, keep an eye on the stress level of that dog over time. If the dog begins to show avoidance, does not want to approach new dogs or begins to change his or her initial greeting behaviors, that particular dog may need a break from his greeting job.

Other daycares schedule a special evaluation day during the evening or weekend when the daycare is not open. This requires more staffing, time and money, but is another option if you prefer a more limited introduction.

During new dog introductions, watch for stress signals and warning signs in the dogs. Note stiffness, high tail carriage, and flattened ears. Watch the response of the dogs that have been attending your daycare for awhile. Sometimes the daycare dog's reaction can be just as instructive as that of the new dog. For example, if you are using a dog that gets along with all dogs, but he is scared of the new dog, that is good information to consider as you conduct the evaluation.

On-Leash Greetings

This is the method of introduction I prefer in daycare. Having both dogs on leash allows you some control if a fight erupts. However, poor leash handling skills on the part of either staff member holding a leash can frustrate the dogs and cause them to lunge at one another. Keeping leashes loose prevents such lunging.

Follow this process for on-leash introductions:

1. Remove all daycare dogs from the introduction area. Take them outside, move them to another section of the daycare or put them in crates.

2. Bring the new dog into the daycare on leash and allow him to explore the room.

3. Introduce one calm, on-leash, daycare dog into the room to meet the new dog.

4. Watch for appropriate greeting behaviors (See box called Greeting Rituals.) Also watch for signs of stress or warning signals. If the dogs do okay, the daycare dog will be taken off leash. Now you have the new dog on leash and the daycare dog off leash.

5. Introduce additional daycare dogs by repeating steps 3 and 4 until you have 5 to 6 daycare dogs off leash with the new dog on leash. At this point, you may consider dropping the leash of the new dog so it drags on the ground. This will prevent the dogs from getting tangled in the leash as they move around. Continue to monitor this small group of dogs. Remove the new dog's leash when he seems relaxed and you are comfortable with his body language and stress level.

Generally speaking, this process should take 3-5 minutes. Afterwards, continue to monitor the dogs for appropriate play and interaction. If the dog seems comfortable and relaxed as the day progresses, you may end up putting him with other dogs.

HOW MANY DOGS FAIL?

If you are screening dogs properly with your application procedures, few dogs will have difficulty meeting the other dogs in your daycare. Ideally, less than 5 percent of your dogs will fail the introduction. If your failure rate exceeds 5 percent then you are wasting valuable staff time and company money. Review your enrollment procedures and try to screen out as many dogs as possible on the phone before you schedule their evaluation. See chapter 3 for more information on the enrollment process.

Off-Leash Greetings

Introducing dogs off leash will occur in very much the same manner as the on-leash introductions except, of course, there are no leashes. The advantage with this method is there is no chance your staff will cause leash frustration in a dog that is pulling on his leash. The disadvantage is that if a fight does occur, you have very little control over the dogs. If you choose to introduce dogs without leashes, your staff needs to be highly skilled in reading canine body language so they can intervene immediately if the dogs do not seem to be getting along. Never toss a new dog into a group of daycare dogs.

One-on-one introductions in the initial period help the new dog acclimate more quickly to the daycare environment.

GREETING RITUALS

Certain rituals commonly occur when two dogs meet. A variation in these rituals can be the first sign of problems between two dogs.

Dogs usually approach one another sideways rather than head on. They will sniff each other's faces and then the rear ends. Humans often find this sniffing routine offensive and attempt to prevent it from occurring. Do not stop the sniffing; this is normal dog greeting behavior.

If one or both dogs freeze and fail to continue the ritual, redirect them by calling them to you. A halt in the sequence can sometimes indicate fear or aggression is brewing. Try not to pull the dogs away with a leash or collar because this can cause frustration and lead to aggression. Instead, use your voice to encourage them to come to you. After a minute or two, allow the dogs to start over.

Dogs that rudely approach other dogs by bounding on their head without stopping to sniff will often be reprimanded by the other dog. This is to be expected, but still needs to be monitored. It is best not to let two dogs meet if either one is overly hyper or stimulated at the time of the meeting. Give them time to settle down before allowing them to meet.

Meeting Through A Fence

Some daycares conduct the initial introduction though a fence. This helps to keep both dogs safe because they are on either side of a fence and cannot make as much contact with one another if they decide to fight. However, the disadvantage is that the natural greeting ritual is hampered because the dogs do not have the freedom to roam around each other to sniff. In addition, some dogs will be frustrated by the barrier and may act more aggressively than if the dog was actually next to them.

If dogs are introduced through a fence, it is still important to have the meetings done one-on-one initially. Letting one new

dog approach a fence full of daycare dogs will be overwhelming to even to the most social dog and may cause high levels of arousal in the daycare.

SUPERVISION IS CONTINUOUS

The monitoring and assessment of a dog does not end once the dog is accepted into daycare. Dog behavior is not static. You will see variations based on the time of day, the dogs in the group on any given day, the changes in environment at home, the changes in different staff members, etc. Dogs can get worse in a daycare. Make sure each dog is leaving the daycare behaviorally better than when he arrived. Constant supervision is the key. Make notes of changes in behavior and be sure to keep the lines of communication with the dog owner open at all times.

TYPES OF INAPPROPRIATE BEHAVIORS

The job of your staff is to monitor the daycare dogs proactively and prevent undesirable behavior from occurring. Teach staff members to watch for early warning signs of potentially dangerous activity and intervene immediately if any of those signs occur. Chapter 6 contains information on early warning signals in dogs. The following guidelines discuss some undesirable behaviors in daycare.

Jumping

Instruct staff members to turn away and ignore a dog that is jumping on them. Petting the dog rewards the jumping and causes the dog to repeat the behavior. Simply ignore the dog and walk away until the dog provides a more appropriate behavior (such as sitting).

The same principle applies to dogs that jump on the door to go out. Do not reward the behavior of jumping on the door by opening the door to let the dog out. Simply wait for the dog to settle down a little (or sit) before opening the door. The dog

will quickly learn that the best way to get attention or to go outdoors is through calm behavior.

Encourage your employees to set up and practice these routines throughout the day. These activities can dramatically improve your staff's day-to-day activity with a group of dogs.

TEACHING SIT AT THE GATE

Does your staff have a few moments of spare time each day? Why not encourage them to teach the dogs to sit at the gate? Several times a day, when no one is in the lobby, practice working with the dogs to teach them to sit at the gate. Once they sit, reward them by letting them proceed through the gate. The dogs are usually happy to play this game even if they are not actually going anywhere. Start with one or two dogs at a time in the morning or afternoon when there are fewer dogs, and gradually introduce each daycare dog to this game. Eventually, teach the dogs to stay in place until you say their name. As the dogs improve, add more distractions such as a person standing on the other side of the fence. This is an excellent game to play to interact with the dogs and teach manners as well.

Mounting

Dogs will often mount one another during daycare. Some dogs will become very aggressive in an attempt to stop the mounting dog and there is a potential for fighting.

If the mounting behavior continues, it is best to prevent a dog from mounting another dog by either physically moving the dog on top or by spraying that dog with a stream of water.

Poop Eating

In general, feces need to be picked up immediately to keep the daycare smelling fresh and clean. Inevitably, though, you will have a dog that adores the taste of poop. Some dogs will even resource guard poop and growl at dogs or people who approach it. If possible, distract the poop-eating dogs anytime

another dog has to go to the bathroom. In the end, immediate cleanup is really the only solution to this problem in a daycare setting.

Barking

Some dogs may bark while they play. Others will bark when customers look into the play area. Still others will fearfully bark at anyone they see. In general, try to prevent a dog from barking excessively. Too much barking may irritate the other dogs as well as the staff and detracts from a fun, pleasant daycare environment.

Not all bark prevention methods will work for all dogs. You will need to experiment to see what works best for each individual dog. The most common bark-stopping strategy is to distract and redirect the barker. If that does not work, try putting a Gentle Leader® on the dog. Although the Gentle Leader®, when worn properly, does not restrict the dog's mouth, it often helps calm the dog so he does not bark out of excitement.

Some dogs will calm down if you leash them and let them walk around with a staff member. If none of these options work, you can attempt to spay a stream of water into the face of the barker. If this is done consistently, and the dog does not like the water, you can sometimes deter the barking behavior.

Sometimes nothing works and the dog must be evaluated for continued attendance at the daycare. Dogs that are barking due to excessive stress may need an environment other than daycare. Additionally, if the barking is obnoxious to the staff, you may consider expelling the dog from daycare to save your staff's sanity.

CONTROLLING INAPPROPRIATE BEHAVIOR

Several methods to control inappropriate behavior can be useful in a daycare setting. Not all methods will work for

every dog. Experiment to see what is most useful for each situation and each particular dog.

Always strive to control behavior in daycare by using a positive approach to intervention. Usually, interrupting the dogs will end most undesirable behavior and allow you to redirect their behavior to more appropriate play. In some cases giving a dog a brief timeout in a crate will help to settle him down enough that he will play more appropriately. Work together with the dog owners to resolve any issues concerning dogs playing in daycare and be sure to inform the clients of any discipline used with their dogs.

MUZZLES IN DAYCARE

Generally, muzzles are not appropriate for daycare dogs. If a dog needs a muzzle he may need training that cannot be properly provided in the daycare. Muzzles used to prevent barking may restrict panting and can cause a dog to overheat. Muzzles used to prevent aggression toward people or dogs, if not used with proper training techniques, can cause frustration in a dog and can cause his aggressive behavior to become worse. In addition, most clients bringing their dog to daycare will be noticeably alarmed if they see a daycare dog wearing a muzzle.

Redirecting the Dog
Redirecting the dog will often control undesirable behavior by changing the context of the dog's play. Simply walking near two dogs playing, calling their names in a high happy tone, or acting silly will usually generate enough attention on you that most dogs will stop what they are doing. This method is the primary means of controlling the dogs in daycare. When redirecting the dogs, the goal is to remain happy and upbeat, not angry.

Calling Timeouts
Timeouts can help deter inappropriate behavior. If a dog is displaying inappropriate behavior, such as barking at another

dog, say, "timeout" and gently lead the dog to a crate. Set a timer for three minutes and then allow the dog to return to the play area. Repeat this sequence for any specific behavior, such as barking, that you would like to deter in an individual dog. Teach your staff to use the timeout effectively. The timeout is not meant to be a place to put the dog when your staff is frustrated. Instead, the timeout is meant to be a structured tool used for safety and training.

Using a Leash or Collar

Some over-stimulated dogs relax when a staff member puts a leash on the dog and takes him for a low-key walk. The leash is being used simply to calm the dog down, not to correct the dog physically. Additionally, a Gentle Leader® headcollar seems to have a calming effect on many dogs. The collar, when worn properly, still allows the dog to open his mouth, eat and drink, but it also helps to settle the dog down. Dogs wearing a Gentle Leader® or leash must be supervised to ensure they do not chew the objects or get tangled in them.

Spraying with Water

For some dogs, a stream of water sprayed in their face serves as a deterrent to inappropriate behavior such as jumping or barking. As with any direct punishment applied to a dog, it must be applied immediately (within 1-3 seconds of the undesirable behavior occurring) and should be effective within four to five tries on a dog. If a dog is sprayed with water more than five times and the inappropriate behavior continues in that episode, then the water is not effective and should stop.

Using a Citronella Collar

A citronella collar is a small mechanical device worn around a dog's neck. If a dog barks, the citronella collar emits a puff of citronella spray in the dog's face. For many dogs, this is a strong deterrent against barking. The citronella collar can be useful with some dogs in daycare. However, there are some drawbacks in a daycare setting. Dogs that are strongly engaged in the barking behavior due to fear or anxiety will

usually not respond to the citronella. They will continue barking despite the spray in their face. Do not use the citronella collar for these dogs because it is not effective. In addition, in a daycare setting, the collar will sometimes go off if a dog near the one wearing the collar barks. This is unfair to the dog with the citronella collar on.

A WORD ABOUT CORRECTIONS

When dealing with inappropriate behavior in dogs, ensure the staff does not inadvertently correct a dog that is not doing anything wrong. For instance, making loud noises (yelling, throw objects, shaking cans with pennies, etc.) to discourage one dog from inappropriate behavior, affects all the dogs in the play area. This type of group punishment should not be used unless absolutely necessary (for instance, in the event of a fight). It is unfair to the non-offending dogs in the room.

Physical punishment of the dogs, by the employees, such as rolling dogs on their back, grabbing them by the scruff of the neck, or pinning them on the ground, should not be used because this teaches the dogs to be wary of the daycare staff. These methods also put your daycare staff at higher risk of being bitten because dogs often defend themselves when being handled in this manner.

Employees will imitate each other. However, the fact that one person is able to safely roll a dog on his back does not mean a new employee will be able to do so. There is a huge liability for you, as the owner of a daycare, if you allow your staff to operate this way.

Any use of punishment needs to be carefully monitored. The staff needs to keep an eye on their emotions and frustration level to ensure the dogs are not being punished excessively or unfairly. Clients need to be aware of any discipline used with the dogs. Most punishment can be avoided by simply teaching your staff to be proactive and redirecting behavior as early as possible.

FIGHTING

The staff's primary job is to identify early warning signs of aggression and intervene before a fight occurs. If you have properly screened dogs for aggression and your staff is diligent in monitoring play, fights will be infrequent.

Plan in advance how the staff needs to react if a fight occurs. Regardless of the method used, the potential for a person to get bitten is great. Proceed with caution in any fighting situation.

If the dogs get into a fight, attempt to break them up by using water first. Try spraying the dogs with water from a squirt bottle, dumping water from a bowl onto the dogs fighting, or spray them with a hose, if available. If that does not work, attempt to make a loud noise (most effective by dropping a metal food bowl on the ground or using an air horn). You can also try using Direct Stop, a product sold by Premier® Pet Products which can sometimes deter the fighting dogs. Sometimes throwing blankets or coats over the fighting dogs can startle them enough to make them stop fighting momentarily.

If none of those measures stops the fight you may need to physically intervene. This is quite risky because many dogs will bite you during a fight. If possible, grab the back legs and quickly pull the dogs apart and let go of them immediately. As soon as the dogs are separated – *crate each dog involved* – no matter which dog started the fight. Check each animal for injuries and treat as necessary. Also check yourself and the staff members who helped break up the fight to see if anyone was injured. Leave the dogs crated for 15 to 20 minutes. When they are released from the crate, supervise them to ensure they do not begin fighting again.

See chapter 8 for more information on dog injuries.

One problem with a fight in a daycare setting is the group mentality that occurs when a fight breaks out. See chapter 6

for more information on the group mentality of dogs involved in a fight.

One of the biggest decisions after a fight is whether to expel the fighting dogs from daycare. Many factors should be taken into consideration in making this decision. If the dogs have been involved in numerous minor incidents in the past, then perhaps they would be best in a pet sitting or daytime boarding situation instead of daycare. If the dogs just seem to dislike one another, then perhaps arranging for them to attend on different days will manage the situation and prevent further altercations. The dog's bite inhibition is also an important consideration in the decision on whether or not to expel the dog. See chapter 6 for information on bite inhibition levels.

When to Tell the Owners
If daycare dogs are involved in a fight, notify the owners as soon as necessary. Obviously, if a dog was injured, the owners will be notified immediately. If the dogs are not injured, you can wait until the owner picks the dog up at the end of the day.

What to Ask Yourself
Anytime there is a serious fight in a daycare, you must review what happened in order to ensure the situation will not happen again. Were there problems with staff supervision? Was the staff negligent in its duties? Were there early warning signs in the dogs that went unnoticed? Was there intervention that should have been used to prevent the fight? Safety is everyone's responsibility and the input of your staff in regard to these questions can help to improve your policies and enhance your facility.

Chapter 8:
Cleanliness, Health, and Safety

Many issues affect the health and safety of both the staff and the dogs in a dog daycare. Good business practices in these areas will allow you to be prepared for the most common situations you may encounter.

CLEANLINESS

Nothing is free of dirt and germs in a daycare. Dogs running and playing together generate a great deal of dust, dander, and dirt. Everything in your daycare is in danger of getting peed, pooped, vomited, and chewed on. You need to ensure a clean and safe environment for the dogs and your staff. Establish and enforce a cleaning schedule to keep the facility looking clean and smelling fresh.

CLEANING SCHEDULE

A detailed daily and weekly cleaning schedule can help ensure the facility always smells fresh and is kept as germ-free as possible. Some items, such as the floor, naptime crates, and water bowls will need daily attention; other items, such as large playground equipment or chairs, may only need weekly cleaning. List everything to be cleaned on the appropriate daily or weekly cleaning schedule so employees can be held accountable for the tasks. It helps to divide the weekly cleaning items and assign a few jobs on each day. This prevents one shift from having to do all the cleaning and spreads the workload throughout the week. For sample daily and weekly cleaning schedules, see appendix A.

FRESH AIR INTAKE

Fresh air intake measures how often the air inside the facility is exchanged with fresh air. Some local governments do not regulate the fresh air intake at all; others regulate it under kennel rules with very specific exchange rates; still others allow a great deal of flexibility so long as some exchange is being made. Be sure to find out if your county requires a certain exchange rate.

CLEANING UP DOG WASTE

Clean up dog accidents immediately. Wipe indoor urine accidents with a mop. Pick up poop immediately and dispose of it in accordance with local laws or regulations. Clean all areas using an appropriate disinfectant.

Outdoors, urine is usually absorbed into the ground or floor covering. However, you will still need to disinfect the area. If the outdoor flooring is non-porous, then you will need to mop and disinfect the area. Outdoors poop can be disposed of in the same manner as indoors.

If you walk dogs outside, instruct the dog walkers to carry bags for immediate pick up of any poop. These bags can be disposed of at the daycare upon returning from the walk.

WHAT DO YOU DO WITH THE POOP?

Many daycares double-bag poop in plastic baggies and toss them in a dumpster. Biodegradable bags are now available for this purpose. These bags cost slightly more than regular plastic bags but are better for the environment. In other daycares, floor drains that connect the daycare plumbing to the city sewage system are installed. You will need to check with your county to determine any special regulations for disposing of poop.

In addition to spot cleaning the floor when accidents occur, clean and disinfect the entire floor twice a day. Often, a cleaning can be done mid-day if the dogs are crated for their naptime. A final cleaning can be done at the end of the day when the dogs have gone home. This twice-daily routine of cleaning and disinfecting will ensure all areas of the floor are kept free of germs, dirt and mud and will prevent a heavy dog smell from taking over your facility.

See appendix B for suggested cleaners, disinfectants and other cleaning supplies.

SHOULD I USE AN AIR DEODORIZER?

Products are available to freshen the smell of the air. These deodorizing systems dispense a scent designed to mask any smells in a dog daycare and can help give the air a pleasant fragrance. Remember their purpose is to hide smells; they are not a substitute for a proper cleaning. Nothing takes the place of good old-fashioned elbow grease in keeping a facility looking and smelling clean. If you use the deodorizing products, be sure you are not simply masking the smell that results when staff members do a less than adequate job cleaning.

MOPS, KENNEL BRUSHES, AND SCRUBBERS

Mops are the most widely used cleaning tools for floors. If your facility does not have a good drainage system, a mop cleans the floor easily and prevents pooling of water. If your floor has a rough surface, replace your mop at regular intervals because it will deteriorate quickly as it rubs against the floor. Vacuum or sweep the floor before mopping to get rid of any dog hair that has piled up.

For daycares with drains in place, a twice-daily hosing, followed by scrubbing the floor with kennel brushes and soapy water will keep the floor clean with a little less labor than regular mopping.

Floor scrubbers offer another option. A floor scrubber is a completely self-contained cleaning machine filled with water and soap. The scrubber is equipped with a pressure system that pushes out soap and water, a scrub brush that scrubs the floor, and a vacuum system that sucks the dirty water back into the machine. Although costly, floor scrubbers allow one person to clean a large room quickly and easily. If you use a floor scrubber, purchase one that holds enough water to allow you to clean your floor on a single tank. It is also helpful to get a scrubber that runs on a rechargeable battery. This allows you to clean the floor even if dogs are in the area without worrying about an electrical cord in the room.

A CASE FOR FLOOR SCRUBBERS

When I moved to my second location, with a play area of approximately 2200 square feet, my staff found it time consuming to clean the floor twice a day. Mopping was not efficient due to our flooring material so we hosed down the floor and used kennel brushes to clean. Then, we rinsed, squeegeed, and air dried the floor. The whole exhausting process took three people approximately 45 minutes to finish. Finally, a staff member proposed the idea of a floor scrubber. We bought an easy-to-use, battery-operated machine that allowed one person to clean the entire room in 15 minutes. Not only did the floor get cleaned more often, but my staff was thrilled. The positive effect on my staff's morale and the overall cleanliness of my facility more than made up for the unexpectedly high cost of the machine. I considered the expense an investment well worth making.

CLEANING CRATES

Clean the insides of all crates any days they are used. If your facility has a drain installed, hose out the crates with soapy water to clean them. If not, then spray the crate with a cleaning agent and wipe out the inside of the crate. Use a disinfectant on the crates after cleaning them. If you are using wire crates, you will need a brush to ensure the wire is

cleaned adequately. If the crates are in the play area, they will get dirty inside and out because the dogs will usually urinate on them and sleep against them. Therefore, you need to clean the outsides of all the crates in the play area as part of your overall cleaning routine.

BEDDING AND TOWELS

Wash all used dog bedding and towels daily to avoid odors and prevent the spread of germs. Soft bedding and towels can be washed in a washing machine for the fastest cleaning. If clients bring their own bedding material or towels, either clean it for them on a routine basis, or ask the client to replace their own bedding with clean material from time to time.

TOOLS FOR CLEANING

The following supplies can be tremendous aids in cleaning your facility. Check out local vendors as well as the resources listed in appendix B for information on these products.
- Mops, brooms, brushes
- Floor scrubbers
- Wet-dry vacuum
- Wysiwash one-stop cleaning system

BOWLS

Stainless steel bowls are the best bowls to use in daycare because they are safe, nonporous, and easy to clean. Plastic bowls are easily destroyed by the dogs and may contain harmful chemicals that can leach into food and water. Wash out the bowls after each use in the daycare using hot soapy water and a safe disinfectant.

DON'T FORGET THE HUMANS

In your quest to keep the daycare clean, do not forget to prevent your staff from spreading germs. Encourage the frequent use of hand sanitizers to prevent the spread of germs between dogs and humans. If any of your staff members work near other animals, such as at a shelter or farm, you might also encourage the use of disinfecting wipes on shoes prior to entering the daycare. This can prevent employees from bringing in germs from other locations.

TOYS

Wash toys daily. Cleaning procedures vary depending on the toy. Soft toys such as rope toys, fleece toys, or tennis balls can be washed in a washing machine and then allowed to air dry or dried in a dryer. Harder plastic or rubber toys can be soaked in a solution of 30 percent bleach to 70 percent water or a safe cleaning solution overnight. Rinse these toys well the next morning prior to re-use in the daycare.

FIRST AID SUPPLIES

Maintain a first aid kit in your daycare with supplies for both humans and dogs. This first aid kit will come in handy for routine care of minor wounds or injuries. In addition to common first aid materials, also include employee injury report forms. These forms may be required by your state for worker's compensation claims. Any human injury that occurs in your daycare, regardless of how minor, should be documented on the employee incident form required by your state's worker's compensation office. This will provide you with insurance against future legal problems if an employee's injury becomes aggravated by the workplace environment.

Document injuries to dogs in the appropriate daycare logbook with a note also entered in the dog's individual file. Be honest with clients and tell them of any injuries that occur with their dog as well as any medical care the dog received at the daycare.

SUGGESTED ITEMS FOR A FIRST AID KIT

Band-aids
Tweezers
Sterile Gauze
Adhesive Tape
Antiseptic Wipes
Various Sizes of Bandages
Instant Ice Pack
Antibiotic Cream
Hydrogen Peroxide
Buffered Aspirin
Benadryl®
Scissors
Thermometer
Plastic Gloves
Styptic Power
Canine Nail Cutters
Petroleum Jelly
Muzzles
List of Emergency Phone Numbers

TAKING TEMPERATURES

A dog's temperature can be taken with the use of a digital rectal thermometer or using new technology of the ear thermometer; the latter is often much faster and easier to use on many dogs. The normal temperature of an adult dog is 101-102 degrees Fahrenheit and slightly higher for a puppy. Consult the veterinarian and notify the dog's owner if a dog's temperature is not within the normal range.

INJURIES

Minor dog injuries in a daycare are unavoidable. Small scrapes and scratches are common and will be treated by the staff using the first aid supplies on hand. More extreme injuries such as puncture wounds, deep cuts and scratches, and multiple injuries on a single dog are not normal and indicate a problem in the daycare supervision or the types of dogs in the daycare environment. Ensure all injuries are documented in the dog's file or a logbook, and tell the client when they pick up the dog. It is always best to personally notify the client rather than have the client find out by talking to other clients, or discovering the injury themselves.

FIRST AID TRAINING

A great way for your staff to get first aid training is by working with a local veterinarian. Offer to teach a short training session to the veterinarian's staff on dog handling skills and the veterinarian can give a short session to your staff on handling minor first aid injuries. This is an excellent way for the veterinarians, technicians, and daycare staff to interact and helps to build a bond between the two businesses. In addition, both staffs get good quality training. The American Red Cross also offers pet first aid classes in many areas.

LIMPING

Dogs, particularly younger puppies and older dogs not used to a high activity level, can tire after even a short bout of playing in a daycare setting. Sometimes, dogs will slam into one another while playing and the impact from this activity can cause temporary limping. Document any limping and inform the client. Dogs that are limping in daycare need to be crated for an hour or two so they can rest. If the limping continues, consult the veterinarian or client to determine if the dog needs be removed from daycare.

Most limping is not life-threatening, but notify a dog's owner if a dog is limping every day. If the limping persists on a daily basis, the owner may need to consult his veterinarian to determine the overall health of the dog.

BEING THE DOG'S ADVOCATE

Consistent limping should be referred to a veterinarian. I once had a young puppy that limped constantly every afternoon. The client told me the puppy never limped at home. However, after several days of this behavior in daycare, I insisted the client take her pet to the veterinarian for a health checkup. They veterinarian discovered the puppy was suffering from early signs of severe hip dysplasia, which ultimately resulted in hip replacement surgery on both hips.

Be sure any dog with injuries has been cleared to attend daycare by a veterinarian who truly understands what it means to play in a daycare setting. I had one veterinarian who told the client that her dysplastic dog could handle *routine daily playing*. The client brought the dog to daycare where the dog was often aggressive when other dogs bumped against her. Ultimately, I called the veterinarian myself and explained how the dogs played in the daycare environment. The veterinarian agreed this was not his definition of *routine activity*, and we removed the dog from the high energy playgroups.

Although the client in this situation did get approval from her veterinarian for the dog to attend daycare, the veterinarian did not understand the nature of play in the daycare environment. You and your staff will often have to be the advocate for the dogs in your care.

Some clients will give buffered aspirin to dogs that are limping. However, do not allow your staff to provide medication to any dogs without written permission from the client or veterinarian. Whenever pain medication is required for a dog in daycare, be careful that the medications are not masking the pain and causing the dog to exacerbate an

already existing condition. If a dog requires pain medication, consider keeping him out of daycare until he feels better.

CUTS AND SCRAPES ON DOGS

It is not uncommon for dogs to suffer mild scrapes and cuts in daycare. Short-haired breeds such as Weimaraners and Dalmatians are particularly prone to these injuries, perhaps because their skin is more sensitive or perhaps simply because the injuries are so much easier to see on the short-haired breeds. Daycare owners often equate these injuries to scraped knees kids inevitably receive when they play on a playground. However, dog owners may be upset when their dogs receive such injuries from daycare. Inform clients before they bring their dogs to daycare that their dogs are likely to have a minor scrape or two; such information can be included in your enrollment application for the client to read. This way you will have informed consent.

BLEEDING

Any cut will bleed, but ear and tail injuries are particularly prone to bleeding. Stop the bleeding with direct pressure and clean all cuts with a hygienic cleaner. If the wound is on the ear or tail, a pressure bandage may need to be applied. Crate the injured dog to lower the activity level. This will help control the bleeding by lowering the heartbeat and blood pressure. In some cases the dog may not be able to play actively for several hours without causing the injury to bleed again. If a bandage is applied to the dog's ear, make sure the client knows what to expect when they pick up the dog. A dog's wrapped head may worry clients because the injury looks so much worse than it really is.

NAIL/PAD INJURIES

Encourage clients to keep their dog's nails short to prevent nail and pad injuries in daycare. If you have someone on staff capable of trimming nails, this is a service you can offer for a small fee.

If a dog cuts or snags a nail, he may need a bandage on his foot. Nail wounds can bleed heavily, so remove a dog with a nail injury from the playgroup until the bleeding is under control. Apply styptic power to the wound and, if necessary, have a veterinarian look at the nail.

The most common paw problem in daycare is sore pads from dogs walking on a hard surface such as pebbles or asphalt. With time, most dogs develop a tougher pad and acclimate to the hard surfaces. However, many dogs that are used to walking on smooth carpet or grass can suffer sore pads and may limp during their first week of daycare. Inform clients of this possibility in advance and ensure your daycare has a soft surface area where dogs can play to minimize problems with sore pads.

TEETHING

It is very common for puppies 4 to 6 months of age to lose their puppy teeth while they are playing. If you see blood on toys or on a dog's neck, often the cause is a lost tooth, especially if you have not seen or heard a fight. A quick check of the younger dogs' mouths will usually reveal which dog lost a tooth. In most cases, the dog will swallow his own tooth which is generally not a problem. However, if you find the tooth, clients usually love seeing it at the end of the day. Some clients will even keep the tooth for their dog's baby book!

INSECT BITES

Insect bites may occur for dogs both inside and outside the facility. Bee stings and spider bites are the most common insect bites. In either cases, the dog may suffer an allergic reaction of swelling in the face or bite location. If you see sudden swelling on a dog with no history of a prior problem, you can usually assume some type of insect bite. Contact your veterinarian to determine the most appropriate medical action. Some veterinarians will recommend a small dose of Benadryl to reduce the swelling and stop the allergic reaction.

Be sure to receive permission from the client or veterinarian before giving any medication.

CONSULTING A VETERINARIAN

My motto is, "When in doubt, take the dog to the veterinarian." I would prefer a veterinarian look at any dog with an injury, even if I know it is minor. Getting a veterinarian's opinion and sharing this opinion with the client enhances your professional image and comforts the client. This extra step can sometimes mean the difference between a client who is upset by an injury and one who understands you have done all you can to make sure his or her dog is safe and well cared for. If you have a good working relationship with your veterinarian, he or she may not even charge much for simple checkups that require no medical treatment. If cost is a concern, a daycare warranty can be beneficial for these kinds of routine checkups. See chapter 3 for more information on the daycare warranty.

TRANSPORTATION SAFETY

If you are providing any transportation for dogs in your daycare, you will need a safe, reliable vehicle with appropriate restraints such as seatbelt harnesses or airline-approved crates. Also be sure you carry adequate insurance coverage for the driver, vehicle, and dogs when you transport them.

STITCHES

Dogs with stitches do not usually attend daycare. The daycare environment is much more active than the home and can cause the stitches to break open or be bothered by another animal. Be sure you know of any surgeries a daycare dog has had and confirm any stitches have been removed or have dissolved before you allow the dog to return to daycare.

CONTAGIOUS ILLNESS

Contagious illnesses among dogs are a fear of all daycare owners. There are several illnesses that are common among dogs, and you can expect to have an outbreak of at least one of these, if not more, at some point during your daycare ownership. Plan for these problems in advance so you are prepared at the earliest sign. Distribute handouts to clients to provide information on various illnesses that may occur.

Canine Cough

Canine cough, sometimes called kennel cough, is an upper respiratory illness in dogs. It is often referred to as a *cold* in dogs because it is similar to a cold in children. It is highly contagious and runs through a group of dogs fairly quickly as colds do in children's classrooms. Canine cough can be minimized through the bordetella vaccination. This is the reason the bordetella vaccination is required by most dog daycares. However, the vaccination does not prevent all cases of canine cough. Unfortunately, many clients believe it does. Explain to your clients that while the bordetella vaccination is helpful in preventing canine cough, it is similar to the flu shot for people. The flu shot helps prevent the flu, but does not stop it completely. Hopefully, those dogs that might contract canine cough will have a less severe form of the disease with a shorter duration if they are healthy and up-to-date on the bordetella vaccination.

The common symptom of canine cough is a dry hacking cough. Remove dogs from daycare if they present this symptom and keep them out of daycare until the cough subsides and a veterinarian confirms the dogs are healthy again. The disease can spread very rapidly. If you have a dog in your daycare that is coughing, then, in all likelihood, the disease has already been spread to other dogs. Notify clients of the effects of canine cough and the symptoms. Also inform them of the possible risk of their dog contracting canine cough during the weeks following first identification of the illness. Obviously, you will take great care to clean the walls and play equipment with a cleaning agent designed to prevent the spread of germs during an outbreak.

TO CLOSE OR NOT TO CLOSE

Some daycare owners close their facility when they have an outbreak of canine cough. This is a personal decision, but is not one I would make. In most cases, canine cough is very treatable and will run its course without major problems. Not all dogs will contract the illness even if exposed. Dogs, like people, have varying degrees of immunity and propensity for illness. Notify all clients whenever a disease has been discovered in the daycare. Although the disease is a known risk, many clients with healthy dogs will continue to bring their dogs to daycare rather than make alternate arrangements for their dogs if the daycare is closed.

Papillomas

Commonly called *puppy warts*, papillomas are unsightly warts that can be found on the insides of a dog's mouth. They are painless and generally do not cause any medical problems. By the time, you see papillomas in a dog, the incubation period has expired and other dogs will likely be affected. The disease is spread through saliva. Most papillomas are found in young dogs and disappear on their own in 4-6 weeks. However, they are a concern to clients because of their location inside the mouth. Provide clients with information on this contagious illness and ask them to keep their dog at home until it clears up. Veterinary care can be handled by the client. Obviously, cleaning will be thorough anytime a contagious outbreak of any illness occurs.

Giardia

Giardia is a parasite that can inhabit a dog's intestine causing a disease known as giardiasis. This disease causes listlessness and diarrhea in dogs and is spread through contaminated water and by dogs licking or eating feces. Because dogs share their water in daycare, an affected dog could carry the disease into the daycare and then pass it on to other dogs though water bowls.

Antibiotics are often used to treat giardia. Ask clients with infected dogs to keep the dog home until the animal is healthy. Giardia can also be spread to humans and cause disease. Proper cleaning procedures as outlined in this chapter are absolutely necessary.

THE LICE LETTER

Looking for a diplomatic, sincere way to notify clients of a contagious outbreak in your daycare? See your local elementary school secretary and borrow a copy of their *lice letter*. These letters are usually well-written, parental letters that provide information about lice when an outbreak occurs in a school. The letter can be excellent template for your own contagious-illness letter.

SAFETY ISSUES
Safety is paramount in a daycare. Everything in the facility must be designed, planned and implemented with safety in mind.

Supply Storage
When planning your daycare, establish a safe dog-proof place to store supplies. Invest in a sturdy cabinet with a lock, a closet for storage, or shelves that can be set high out of animal reach. Instruct your staff to store cleaning supplies immediately after each use to prevent accidental ingestion or spillage by a dog in daycare. Look for dog-friendly, nontoxic cleaning products as well.

Access to the Playroom
For safety reasons, do not allow non-employees to enter the play area during daycare. Dogs will usually jump on strangers entering the room and you assume a big liability risk if you allow visitors or clients into an area where dogs are playing off-leash. In addition, introducing a new person to a group of dogs can cause arousal in the room and increases the potential for a fight. Finally, not all dogs enjoy

the company of strangers and some can become defensive or protective when an unknown person enters. The safest policy is one in which only staff members have access to the playroom.

Walking Dogs

Waking dogs outside is inherently risky and can be avoided by having a safely enclosed outdoor area or by operating a completely indoor facility. However, if this is not possible, keep walks as safe as possible by instituting clear policies for the dog walkers.

For safety, use a collar with an escape-proof design such as the Premier® Collar or the Lupine® Combo Collar. Dogs that pull can be safely walked with either a head collar or special body harness, such as the Premier® Easy-Walk™ harness. Walk the dogs in a low-traffic area where there is little potential to encounter other people or dogs.

Discourage strangers from petting the daycare dogs while they are being walked because the dogs may not tolerate a stranger's attention, and many dogs are harder to control around other people. If someone wants to pet the dogs, politely decline the offer and tell the person the dogs do not belong to you. Staff members walking dogs should keep the leash over their wrist at all times while walking. For an additional measure of safety, have staff members walk the dogs with a double leash system. The second leash can be attached around the staff member's waist for added security.

Toy Safety

Remember to check toys frequently for wear and tear. Throw away toys that are fraying, breaking, or crumbling. Replace tennis balls that become soft. Ensure the toy size is adequate for the dogs playing with them. Toys that are too small can be choking hazards for larger dogs. Avoid toys that can be chewed apart easily because these can be ingested by dogs and cause an intestinal blockage.

Beds, Towels, and Blankets

Not all daycares use bedding, towels or blankets. If you do use these items, keep an eye on dogs that chew things because the material can be ingested and cause the dog to get sick.

Collars

You will need to determine whether or not you want the dogs in your daycare to wear collars. Collars can be dangerous because a dog can get his jaw stuck in another dog's collar. If this happens, the dogs panic and twist, causing the collar to tighten and possibly strangle the dog. When this occurs, it is very difficult to untangle the dogs. The collar is generally so tight you can not easily unsnap it either. If this is a risk in your facility, ensure you have easy access to good quality scissors to cut off a dog's collar.

If you must use collars for identification of the dogs, consider using a break-away collar. These collars are designed to unhook if they are snagged on something. Keep in mind that these collars are not useful if you try to move a dog by the collar because the collar will unhook when you grab it. Carrying a slip-lead will allow you to move the dogs safely if you are not using collars.

Metal collars of any kind are dangerous in a playgroup and need to be removed before allowing the dog to attend daycare.

EVACUATION PLANS

Develop an adequate evacuation plan for your daycare. The evacuation plan must be understood, displayed and frequently rehearsed by the staff in the event of an emergency. You will need a plan for fire as well as a plan for natural disasters common to your area. At least twice a year, hold evacuation drills to ensure your staff is adequately prepared for an emergency.

If you have to leave the building in a hurry, you may not have time to print a list of client data. Therefore, a current contact list containing all client information and emergency contact numbers must be readily available at all times. This list ensures you can contact your clients and provide them with information about the locations of the dogs.

If you plan to crate all the dogs in the case of a natural disaster, you need to ensure enough crates are available. If you are going to take the dogs outside the building, you will need enough leashes. Remember, not all clients will bring their dog on a suitable leash, and you may not have time to grab each leash brought in by a client. Therefore, have enough spare leashes available for daycare use located in a convenient place in the event of an emergency.

Appendix A
Sample Forms and Documents

This appendix contains sample forms and other documents designed to help a daycare owner operate a safe and successful daycare. All the material provided can be tailored to suit the needs of the individual daycare and are provided as a sample.

Sample forms included:
- Enrollment Cover Letter
- Enrollment Application
- Owner Liability Waiver and Health Certification
- Reservation Form
- Payment Pass
- Report Card
- Serious Incident Report
- Office Area Daily Responsibility Sheet
- Office Area Weekly Responsibility Sheet
- Play Area Daily Responsibility Sheet
- Play Area Weekly Responsibility Sheet
- Job Descriptions
- Employment Application Disclaimer
- Telephone Flowchart

SAMPLE ENROLLMENT COVER LETTER

ABC Daycare Letterhead

Dear Dog Owner,

Thank you for your recent inquiry about dog daycare. ABC Daycare is committed to providing a safe, fun and stimulating social environment for your pet during weekday business hours. At dog daycare, your pet will not be crated for long hours, but will enjoy supervised playtime with other pets and our friendly staff.

Enclosed, you will find information and forms you need to register your pet for our services. There is a one-time, $XX.XX non-refundable application processing fee for each pet.

To enroll, simply fill out the enclosed forms and return them to ABC Daycare at {address} along with proof of vaccinations and a check or money order for $XX.XX for each pet. You may enroll through the mail, via internet {website address} or if you prefer, you may drop your application off in person. Once we receive your enrollment form, proof of vaccinations and enrollment fee, we will screen your paperwork and call to schedule a time when we can meet your pet.

If you have any questions, please feel free to contact us at (XXX) XXX-XXXX or stop by the Center to visit our facility. Our office is opened Monday through Friday from 6:30 a.m. to 7:00 p.m. We look forward to seeing you and your pet.

ABC Daycare

SAMPLE ENROLLMENT APPLICATION

ABC Daycare Letterhead

FOR OFFICE USE ONLY
Enrollment Form_____ Enrollment Fee_____ Shots_____
Staff Screened_____ Computer Entry_____ First Day_____
NOTES:

EMERGENCY CONTACT INFORMATION

Owner Information
Name: _____
Address: _____
EMAIL:_____
Home Phone: _____Work Phone: _____

Emergency Contact
Name: _____
EMAIL:_____
Home Phone: _____Work Phone: _____

Pet Information
Name: _____Breed: _____ Sex:_____
Birthdate:_____ Weight: _____

Veterinarian
Name: _____
Address: _____
EMAIL:_____
Phone: _____Fax:_____

Pet Personality Profile

Owner's Last Name: _____
How did you hear about ABC Daycare?_____
Dog's Name: _____Date you acquired dog: _____
Is dog spayed/neutered? _____ At what age was it done?___
Where did you get your dog? _____

If adopted, do you have any knowledge of your dog's past history? _____

Does your dog like children?_____

How does your dog behave around children?

_____

Are there other animals in your household? If so, please list type, sex and age of each:

_____

How does your dog get along with other resident animals?

_____

Health/Grooming

Does your dog have a problem with fleas? __Allergies?___

Does your dog have hip dysplasia? _____If yes, what restrictions need to be placed on your dog's activities or movements?_____

Does your dog like to be brushed? _____

How does your dog react to having his/her nails clipped?

_____

Does your dog have any sensitive areas on his/her body?

_____

Where are your dog's favorite petting spots? _____

Behavior

Does your dog act afraid of any specific items or noises? If so, please explain: _____

How does your dog react to strangers coming into your home or yard? _____

Does your dog ever bark or growl at anyone passing outside your home or yard? _____

Are there any kinds of people your dog automatically fears or dislikes? _____

Are there any kinds of dogs your dog automatically fears or dislikes? _____

How does your dog react to puppies? _____

Has your dog ever:

Growled at someone?_____ What were the circumstances:

_____

Bitten someone?_____What were the circumstances:

_____

Does your dog have any problems in any of the following areas: (if so, please explain)

Mouthiness: _____ Housetraining: _____

Barking: _____ Digging: _____

Jumping: _____ Other: _____

Has your dog ever growled or snapped at anyone who has taken his/her food or toys away from him/her? _____

What were the circumstances: _____

Has your dog ever shared his/her food or toys with other animals? _____

Does your dog play with any toys? _____ If yes, what kind of toys does your dog like and what games does he/she play? _____

Does your dog play with other dogs? _____

Has your dog ever had any formal obedience training? _____

If yes, when and where? _____

What commands does your dog know? _____

_____

Other comments about your dog which you feel might be helpful: _____

Dog Daycare General Information and Policies

The purpose of ABC Dog Daycare Center ("Center") is to provide a safe, fun and stimulating social environment for dogs during weekday business hours. To ensure the safety and health of your pet and our other guests, we require all guests to comply with the following rules and regulations:

AGE: All dogs must be at least 12 weeks of age or older.

SEX: All dogs 7 months or older must be spayed or neutered.

SHOTS: All dogs must have up-to-date vaccinations. Owners must submit written proof of DHLPP and Bordetella vaccinations. Rabies is required for puppies over 4 months of age.

HEALTH: All dogs must be in good heath. Owners will certify their dog(s) are in good health and have not been ill with a communicable condition in the last XX days. Upon

admission, all dogs must be free from any condition which could potentially jeopardize other guests. Dogs that have been ill with a communicable condition in the last XX days will require veterinarian certification of heath to be admitted or readmitted.

BEHAVIOR: All dogs must be non-aggressive and not food or toy protective. Owners will certify their dogs have not harmed or shown any aggressive or threatening behavior towards any person or any other dog(s). Please remember: your pet will be spending time with other pets and the safety and health of all animals is our main concern.

APPLICATION: All dogs must have a complete, up-to-date and approved application on file. There is a one-time, $XX.XX non-refundable application screening fee for each pet.

FEES: Fees are based on a pass plan. A pass is valid for 6 months from date of purchase. Additional dogs are $X.00 per day, per dog.
   1-day pass: $XX.00
   5-day pass: $XX.00 ($XX.00 per day)
   10-day pass: $XXX.00 ($XX.00 per day)
   20-day pass $XXX.00 ($XX.00 per day)
   Additional dogs: $X.00 per day per additional dog

DAYS AND HOURS: Monday through Friday from 6:30 a.m. to 7:00 p.m. The Center is not an overnight facility. Staff goes off duty at 7:00 p.m. and there is a $1.00 per minute charge for any pet left after 7:00 p.m.

RESERVATIONS: Required. Cancellations with less than 24 hours notice will be charged full fees.

SAMPLE OWNER LIABILITY WAIVER AND HEALTH CERTIFICATION

OWNER AGREEMENT

I, _____, hereby certify that my dog(s): _____ is/are in good health and has/have not been ill with any communicable condition in the last XX days. I further certify that my dog(s) has/have not harmed or shown aggressive or threatening behavior towards any person or any other dog. I have read and understand the following:

1. I understand that I am solely responsible for any harm caused by my dog(s) while my dog(s) is/are attending ABC Daycare Center ("Center").

2. I further understand and agree that in admitting my dog(s) to the Center, ABC Daycare's staff have relied on my representation that my dog(s) is/are in good health and has/have not harmed or shown aggressive or threatening behavior towards any person or any other dog.

3. I further understand and agree that ABC Daycare Center and their staff and volunteers, will not be liable for any problems that develop, provided reasonable care and precautions are followed, and I hereby release them of any liability of any kind whatsoever arising from my dog's/dogs' attendance and participation at the Center.

4. I further understand and agree that dogs can sometimes receive minor cuts and scratches at daycare and any problems that develop with my dog(s) will be treated as deemed best by staff and volunteers of ABC Daycare Center, at their sole discretion, and that I assume full financial responsibility for any and all expenses involved.

I certify that I have read and understand the policies of the Center as set forth on the preceding pages and that I have

read and understand the conditions, and statements of this agreement, including the following:

FEES: Fees are based on a pass plan. A pass is valid for 6 months from date of purchase.

DAYS AND HOURS: Monday through Friday from 6:30 a.m. to 7:00 p.m. The Center is not an overnight facility. Staff goes off duty at 7:00 p.m. and there is a $1.00 per minute charge for any pet left after 7:00 p.m.

RESERVATIONS: Required. Cancellations with less than 24 hours notice will be charged full fees.

Dated: _____

Signature of Owner:_____

RESERVATION FORM

Date:

Paid		Name	Transport	Grooming	Notes
	1				
	2				
	3				
	4				
	5				
	6				
	7				
	8				
	9				
	10				
	11				
	12				
	13				
	14				
	15				
	16				
	17				
	18				
	19				
	20				
	21				
	23				
	23				
	25				

This is a manual form to use for one day of daycare. Annotate the information as needed for each dog.

SAMPLE PAYMENT PASS

10-DAY PASS

Dog's Name: Date Purchased:
Owner: Exp. Date:
Cost:

1 _____   6 _____
2 _____   7 _____
3 _____   8 _____
4 _____   9 _____
5 _____   10 _____

SAMPLE REPORT CARD

ABC DAYCARE REPORT CARD

Report card for _____ Date:_____

I had a GREAT day at ABC Daycare. I played
_____ with my friends
_____and _____. _____ took
very good care of me and wanted you to know
_____.
I'm looking forward to coming back soon.

This form can be used to notify owners of fun activities during the day. It can also be used to notify owners of any health or behavioral concerns.

SAMPLE SERIOUS INCIDENT REPORT

Employee name: _____

Date of indent: _____

Time and place of incident: _____

Was employee working at time of incident?_____

Was employee paid full wages for day of incident? _____

Date injury reported:_____ To whom?_____

Witnesses: _____

Machine, tool, object or dog causing incident:_____

_____

Describe fully how incident occurred:

Describe nature of injury or illness that resulted from incident:

Describe medical treatment administered:

Place where employee was treated for medical injuries:

Did employee return to work? _____ When? ____

Signature of employee: _____

SAMPLE OFFICE AREA DAILY RESPONSIBILITY SHEET
Office Area Opening Responsibilities
(6:30 a.m. – 11:30 a.m.)

DATE:_____OPENING SUPERVISOR:_____

The opening supervisor is responsible for ensuring these duties are completed each day. The person who actually does the job will initial the form. Note that the job responsibilities are listed in the order they should be done. The duties are all standardized and measurable so everyone can do them in the same manner.

Super-
Visor   Staff

_____   _____   Arrive at least 10 minutes prior to shift
_____   _____   Lock door to keep clients out until
                opening
_____   _____   Check messages on answering machine
_____   _____   Read logbook entries from previous day
_____   _____   Unlock door promptly at 6:30 a.m.
_____   _____   Greet guests, annotate payment cards
_____   _____   Make logbook note of special dog needs
_____   _____   Photos of any new dogs
_____   _____   Put lunches in bowls with crate cards as
                dogs arrive
_____   _____   Complete admin duties (mailing, phone
                calls, etc)
_____   _____   Put crate cards on naptime crates
_____   _____   Put lunches, treats and blankets in crates
_____   _____   Review logbook for any action items
_____   _____   Annotate logbook with information
                needed by the next shift (i.e. unpaid
                accounts, canceled reservations, owner
                concerns, etc.)

Office Area Mid-Day Responsibilities
(11:30 a.m. – 12:30 p.m.)

Super-
Visor   Staff

_____   _____   Check change fund – get change if needed (making sure at least one $10 bill, one $5 bill and five $1 bills as well as change)

_____   _____   Complete administrative duties

_____   _____   Call to confirm tomorrow's appointments

_____   _____   Straighten office area and lobby

_____   _____   Spot clean windows and doors

_____   _____   Clean coffee pot (when needed)

_____   _____   Complete weekly responsibilities

Office Area Closing Responsibilities
(1:30 p.m. – 7:00 p.m.)

DATE:_____CLOSING SUPERVISOR:_____

The closing supervisor is responsible for ensuring these duties are completed each day. The person who actually does the job will initial the form. Note that the job responsibilities are listed in the order they should be done. The duties are all standardized and measurable so everyone can do them in the same manner.

Super-
Visor   Staff

_____   _____   Ensure 11:30-12:30 activities are done

_____   _____   Read logbook entries from morning

_____   _____   Review reservations for special needs of dogs – ensure they have been done

_____   _____   Double check all payment cards for day (correct discrepancies)

_____   _____   Put uneaten food back in dog bins

_____   _____   Write report cards for dogs that didn't eat

_____   _____   Re-file crate cards

Super-Visor	Staff	
_____	_____	Pull all payment cards, crate cards for next day
_____	_____	Prepare next day's transportation roster
_____	_____	Ensure all dogs have a bin for the next day
_____	_____	Empty trash in front office and lounge
_____	_____	Straighten lobby and office
_____	_____	Sweep and mop office, lobby and lounge
_____	_____	Remove checks and cash over $30 from cash box and place in safe
_____	_____	Place credit card receipts in safe
_____	_____	Check answering machine for messages
_____	_____	Back up database
_____	_____	Complete all admin duties
_____	_____	Ensure office and lobby are organized and clean
_____	_____	Turn off office lights, set alarm and lock door

SAMPLE OFFICE AREA WEEKLY RESPONSIBILITY SHEET
**Office Weekly Responsibilities
(complete between 12:30 p.m. and 1:30 p.m.)**

The opening supervisor is responsible for ensuring these duties are completed each day. The person who actually does the job will initial the form.

DATE: MONDAY,   **SUPERVISOR:** _____

Super-
Visor   Staff

_____   _____   Clean window sills
_____   _____   Dust office and lobby
_____   _____   Water plants in office
_____   _____   Other

DATE: TUESEDAY,   **SUPERVISOR:** _____

Super-
Visor   Staff

_____   _____   Straighten storage cabinet in office
_____   _____   Wipe down food preparation area with
                cleaning solution
_____   _____   Spot clean all doors and walls in office
                and lobby
_____   _____   Other

DATE: WEDNESDAY,   **SUPERVISOR:** _____

Super-
Visor   Staff

_____   _____   Clean lobby windows and doors with
                Windex
_____   _____   Sweep behind bins
_____   _____   Other

DATE: THURSDAY,   **SUPERVISOR:** _____

Super-
Visor   Staff

_____   _____   Spot clean office and lobby
_____   _____   Dust pictures and insides of bins in
                         lobby (1/2 of them)
_____   _____   Other

DATE: FRIDAY,   **SUPERVISOR:** _____

Super-
Visor   Staff

_____   _____   Dust inside of bins in lobby (other 1/2)
_____   _____   Other

SAMPLE PLAY AREA DAILY RESPONSIBILITY SHEET
Play Area Opening Responsibilities
(6:30 a.m. – 11:30 a.m.)

DATE:_____OPENING SUPERVISOR:_____

The opening supervisor is responsible for ensuring these duties are completed each day. The person who actually does the job will initial the form. Note that the job responsibilities are listed in the order they should be done. The duties are all standardized and measurable so everyone can do them in the same manner.

Super-Visor	Staff	
_____	_____	Enter building 5 minutes prior to shift
_____	_____	Put filled mop buckets into the play areas
_____	_____	Put water buckets out for dogs
_____	_____	Read logbook entries from previous day
_____	_____	Note special instructions for dogs today
_____	_____	Ensure there are 2 crates in each play area
_____	_____	Change collars on all dogs in double gate area
_____	_____	Take dogs out to bathroom as soon as they arrive
_____	_____	Separate dogs by size and temperament as needed
_____	_____	Spot clean as needed
_____	_____	Take photos of any new dogs
_____	_____	Change mop bucket any time it's dirty
_____	_____	Refill water buckets often
_____	_____	Sweep floor of dog hair often
_____	_____	Clean all crates in play areas
_____	_____	Put dogs down for naps at 11:30 a.m.

Play Area Mid-Day Responsibilities
(11:30 a.m. – 12:30 p.m.)

Super-
Visor   Staff

_____   _____   Scrub floor with floor scrubber
_____   _____   Rinse out water compartment of scrubber
_____   _____   Clean out sink of dog hair
_____   _____   Manually clean hair along fence and walls
_____   _____   Refill all water buckets
_____   _____   Refill all spray bottles
_____   _____   Change all mop buckets
_____   _____   Sweep, mop and empty trash in bathroom
_____   _____   Set indoor trash aside and put new bag in
_____   _____   Complete weekly responsibilities

Play Area Closing Responsibilities
(1:30 p.m. – 7:00 p.m.)

DATE:_____CLOSING SUPERVISOR:_____

The closing supervisor is responsible for ensuring these duties are completed each day. The person who actually does the job will initial the form. Note that the job responsibilities are listed in the order they should be done. The duties are all standardized and measurable so everyone can do them in the same manner.

Super-
Visor   Staff

_____   _____   Ensure 11:30-12:30 activities are done
_____   _____   Take dogs out of crates and take outside
_____   _____   Remove bowls from crates
_____   _____   Return uneaten food to front office with
                 dog's crate card in bowl
_____   _____   Remove all crate cards from crate doors
                 and return to office
_____   _____   Clean all crates used

Super-Visor	Staff	
_____	_____	Sweep and mop nap room
_____	_____	Straighten shelves in nap room
_____	_____	Wash bowls
_____	_____	Check laundry basket (wash towels if needed)
_____	_____	Note special instructions on today's list
_____	_____	Spot clean as needed
_____	_____	Refill water buckets often
_____	_____	Put up next day's list of dogs
_____	_____	Wipe down all doors inside playroom
_____	_____	Hose down blacktop after dogs come back inside
_____	_____	Check amount of baggies (put up more if needed)
_____	_____	Put away bottles, excess items in play area
_____	_____	Sweep floor often
_____	_____	Use scrubber to clean floor
_____	_____	Empty scrubber
_____	_____	Clean sink of hair
_____	_____	Put mops in bleach to soak overnight
_____	_____	Fill spray bottles
_____	_____	Inventory supplies, note items needed
_____	_____	Take indoor and outdoor trash to dumpster
_____	_____	Lock back door and hang key on fence
_____	_____	After all dogs leave, wash buckets

SAMPLE PLAY AREA WEEKLY RESPONSIBILITY SHEET
Play Area Weekly Responsibilities
(complete between 12:30 p.m. and 1:30 p.m.)

The naptime supervisor is responsible for ensuring these duties are completed each day. The person who actually does the job will initial the form.

DATE: MONDAY,   **SUPERVISOR:** _____

Super-
Visor   Staff

_____   _____   Clean bathroom with cleanser
_____   _____   Wipe down all walls with cleaner
_____   _____   Other *

DATE: TUESDAY,   **SUPERVISOR:** _____

Super-
Visor   Staff

_____   _____   Straighten storage area
_____   _____   Mop and squeegee in trash area
_____   _____   Other *

DATE: WEDNESDAY,   **SUPERVISOR:** _____

Super-
Visor   Staff

_____   _____   Clean bathroom with cleanser
_____   _____   Wipe down all play equipment inside
_____   _____   Wipe down all resin chairs inside
_____   _____   Other *

DATE: THURSDAY,   **SUPERVISOR:** _____

Super-
Visor   Staff

_____   _____   Wipe down play equipment outside
_____   _____   Wipe down resin chairs outside
_____   _____   Other *

DATE: FRIDAY,   **SUPERVISOR:** _____

Super-
Visor   Staff

_____   _____   Move all naptime crates, sweep and mop
_____   _____   Wash all fleece blankets, collars, leashes
_____   _____   Other *

*Wash dog toys with bleach/water or laundry when used

SAMPLE JOB DESCRIPTIONS

Daycare Manager

Directly responsible to the daycare owner for the proper functioning of all daycare operations. Ensures all staff members working in daycare are properly trained and supervised. Ensures the daycare staff understands policies, procedures and regulations pertaining to dogs in daycare. Responsible for ensuring the daycare staff makes proper notes of any problems encountered in daycare, to include dogs who do not eat well, have diarrhea, vomiting or other problems. Ensures the daily schedule for naptime and feeding is properly maintained and ensures standards of cleanliness are followed by all members of the staff. Determines the suitability of dogs in daycare. Prepares listing of dog problems or concerns and keeps up-to-date information on all dog concerns. Responsible for updating photographs and comment cards on dogs in the daycare as needed. Works with the Office Manager to ensure proper daycare forms and databases are maintained. Monitors feeding, playing, and walking of dogs in conjunction with needs of the clients. Meets with owners as needed to discuss overall behavior of dogs attending daycare. Ensures the overall operations of the daycare are conducted professionally.

Daycare Staff

Works under the direct supervision of the Daycare Manager to ensure daycare dogs are properly cared for, fed and supervised. Monitors the overall activities of the dogs in daycare. Responsible for ensuring proper dogs play together and monitors playing to prevent injuries or fights. Ensures standards of cleanliness are maintained in the play area which includes cleaning up after any accidents, sweeping and moping and keeping dogs clean. Responsible for following naptime schedules and feeding schedules for all dogs attending daycare and supervising the walking of any dogs that need to be taken outside. Responsible for cleaning crates, toys and other play equipment each day.

Office Manager

Directly responsible for all client relations and the overall administrative matters of the facility. Reports directly to the daycare owner and is the direct supervisor for the driver. Responsible for hiring/firing direct subordinates and conducting performance reviews in conjunction with the owner. Works in conjunction with the financial/legal supervisor to assist in billing and legal concerns as directed by the owner. Works directly with subordinates to ensure all responsible areas are operated in a timely and professional manner. Responsible for direct contact with clients and maintains personal interaction with potential and current clients. Responsible for answering client concerns as needed as well as handling billing and payment problems. As first contact with clients, this person must understand all policies and procedures at the facility and must have excellent personal skills to interact in a professional and efficient manner. Must understand and be able to explain all services offered. Maintains current information on all referrals in the database in order to track client information. Monitors the overall operation of the administrative office and ensures it is kept organized and functional. Responsible for ensuring adequate supplies and copies of printed material are on hand for office work and advertising in coordination with all subordinate sections. Prepares and distributes routine paperwork as directed by the owner. Reviews work schedule for all employees to ensure adequate staffing is accomplished. Works with the Daycare Manager to ensure all daily client needs are handled properly and annotated as needed.

Financial/Legal Supervisor

Reports directly to the Office Manager. Responsible for preparing monthly income statements and detailed general ledger each month. Responsible for quarterly income statements, to include unemployment taxes, retail taxes, and other payments required. Responsible for payroll computations and tax withholding figures. Responsible for filing annual tax forms for IRS and state taxes. Also provides counseling on financial status of the business and provides

financial statements as needed for outside sources. Legal advisor is responsible for ensuring legal concerns of the business are properly handled. Legal concerns include, but are not limited to: proper insurance, proper waivers, proper forms for business entity and licensing, and other legal forms needed to protect the business.

Driver

Works directly for the Office Manager. Responsible for making runs as needed to pick up/drop off copies, take forms and brochures to veterinarian offices, pick up/drop off dogs at various veterinarian offices and pick up/drop off dogs at owner's homes as needed. Driver will use the company vehicle and must maintain an excellent driving record. Responsible for maintaining the company vehicle in excellent state of readiness. As directed, will conduct maintenance checks and cleaning of vehicle or take vehicle to receive required maintenance. If no active driving runs are required, driver will assist the Office Manager as necessary or may be used to assist in the daycare area.

EMPLOYMENT APPLICATION DISCLAIMER
(Courtesy of Molly's Country Kennels in Landsdale, PA.)

A disclaimer such as this can be used to explain the job responsibilities and expectations to prospective new hires.

We would like to thank you for showing an interest in working here. However, we have found in the past that many people do not have a very realistic view of what working in a place like this involves. Please read this letter carefully.

First, you need to understand that the primary purpose of this facility is to take care of other people's pets during the day. This business is seasonal in nature, you can expect your hours or days to vary according to our needs. We realize that working under these conditions can be pretty difficult for some people, but that is the nature of the business and your DEPENDABILITY in this area is critical. If you don't think you can be that flexible, you should really seek employment elsewhere.

If you do not have a genuine love of animals, you do not need to be here. But keep in mind that we are seeking people who are mature enough to understand and accept the responsibilities we will place on them. You are NOT going to be paid to sit around and play with cute little puppies all day. Someone has to clean up after them, feed them, administer medications, and see to their comfort and security. This requires a great deal of hard work and dedication.

While working here you will be exposed to: filth, loud noises, harsh chemicals, a variety of parasites and zoonoses (medical ailments that people can acquire from animals) and the ever present risk of being bitten, scratched or mauled. These are the potential hazards you face and accept by working here.

You should also know that with very few exceptions there are NO specialists here. You will be expected to perform any task we require of you. We will try to make the best use of your

skills and experience, but don't expect to be exempt from the more mundane and unpleasant chores that need to be performed. Floors need to be mopped, cages cleaned, and trash cans emptied. If you get ill at the idea of cleaning up diarrhea or vomit, then you are in the wrong place. If you can't pick up a 50 pound bag of food by yourself, this isn't the right place for you. If you are allergic to animal hair or sensitive to chemicals, now is the time to leave.

We are looking for mature, responsible people. You must be reliable, patient, intelligent, and capable of independent action. If you have to be constantly supervised, or if you cannot find things to do on your own, then you are not the person we are looking for.

We take our profession very seriously. If you wish to work here, then you must too. If you can make this commitment, then proceed to fill out your job application.

Employee Signature   Date

SAMPLE TELEPHONE FLOWCHART

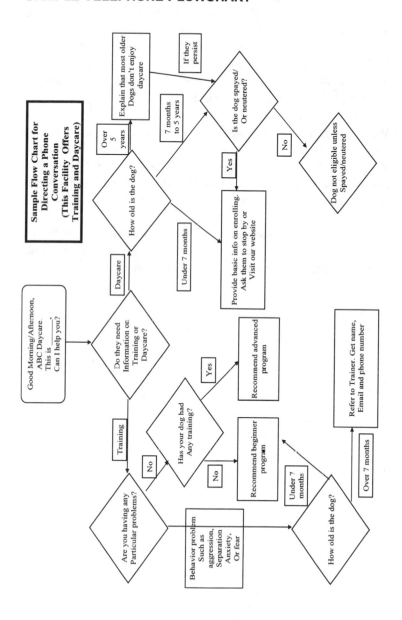

Sample Flow Chart for Directing a Phone Conversation (This Facility Offers Training and Daycare)

Good Morning/Afternoon, ABC Daycare. This is _____, Can I help you?

Do they need Information on: Training or Daycare?

- Daycare → How old is the dog?
  - Over 5 years → Explain that most older Dogs don't enjoy daycare → If they persist → Is the dog spayed/Or neutered?
  - 7 months to 5 years → Is the dog spayed/Or neutered?
    - Yes → Provide basic info on enrolling. Ask them to stop by or Visit our website
    - No → Dog not eligible unless Spayed/neutered
  - Under 7 months → Provide basic info on enrolling. Ask them to stop by or Visit our website

- Training → Are you having any Particular problems?
  - No → Has your dog had Any training?
    - Yes → Recommend advanced program
    - No → Recommend beginner program
  - Behavior problem Such as aggression, Separation Anxiety, Or fear → How old is the dog?
    - Under 7 months → Recommend beginner program
    - Over 7 months → Refer to Trainer. Get name, Email and phone number

Appendix B
Resources

BUSINESS PLANNING RESOURCES

American Pet Products Manufacturing Association (APPMA)
http://www.appma.org/
Promotes pet ownership and the pet product industry. Gathers statistics on pet manufacturing products and services.

Business Plan Pro
http://www.paloalto.com/
Software designed for business planning. Current versions include a sample business plan for a dog daycare.

Humane Society of the United States (HSUS)
http://www.hsus.org/
Provides information on pet ownership statistics and humane care of all animals.

Market Research Website
http://www.export.gov/marketresearch.html

Small Business Administration (SBA)
http://www.sba.gov/
For information on all aspects of business ownership from start-up to growth, including financial concerns. Links to numerous counselors and development centers to assist small business owners.

U.S. Patent and Trademark Office
http://www.uspto.gov/
Provides a searchable database for service marks, trademarks, and business names

U.S. Pet Ownership and Demographics Source Book
http://www.avma.org/membshp/marketstats/sourcebook.asp
This is a comprehensive survey of pet owners and pet population demographics. It is available from the American Veterinary Medical Association

CLEANING PRODUCTS
Household cleaning products can be found locally. Other products can be ordered from pet product companies
- A-33 Dry
- Bleach
- Oda-ban
- Quat 256 Disinfectant Cleaner
- Roccal-D Disenfectant
- Simple Green
- Wysiwash http://www.wysiwash.com/

DOG BEHAVIOR AND BODY LANGUAGE RESOURCES
Books on canine body language, learning theory, and training. Most books and videos available through Dogwise at http://www.dogwise.com. Dog-related seminars available at http://www.puppyworks.com/

- Calming Signals by Turid Rugaas
- Culture Clash by Jean Donaldson
- Dog Behavior Pamphlets (especially Fighting and Biting) by Ian Dunbar
- Dog to Dog Aggression Video by Sue Sternberg
- Dog Language by Roger Abrantes

- Excel-erated Learning by Pamela Reid
- A Guide to Choosing Your Next Dog From the Shelter by Sue Sternberg
- How to Own and Operate a Dog Daycare Video by Robin Bennett
- The Other End of the Leash by Patricia McConnell
- The Power of Positive Training by Pat Miller
- Temperament Testing for Dogs in Shelters by Sue Sternberg

FENCING/KENNEL DESIGN
Clark Cages
http://www.clarkcages.com/

Design Learned Inc.
http://www.designlearned.com/

Horst Custom Animal Enclosures
http://www.horstcompany.com/

Mason Company
http://www.masonco.com/

FLOORING
Dog Kennel Floors
http://www.dogkennelfloors.com/

Golden Look International
http://www.goldenlook.com/

Kennel Deck
http://www.kenneldeck.com/

Kennel Komfort
http://sharshootsphotos.tripod.com/LRP/index.html

RB Rubber
http://www.rbrubber.com/

Tuflex Rubber Flooring
http://www.tuflex.com/

HUMAN RESOURCE INFORMATION
Jian ®
http://www.jian.com/index.html
Software for businesses. The Employee Manual Builder and
Agreement Builder are excellent.

INSURANCE COMPANIES
Kennel Pak
http://www.kennelpak.com/

Mourer Foster
http://www.mourerfoster.com/
Attn: Dennis Stowers
1-800-686-2663

MERCHANT SERVICES
Sterling Payment Technologies, LLC
Attn: Ed Connor
(703) 670-3882

PAYROLL SERVICES
Paycycle
http://www.paycycle.com/
Provides payroll processing, tax filing and other business
services.

Primepay
http://www.primepay.com/
Provides payroll processing, tax filing and other business services.

PET SUPPLIES (COLLARS, CRATES LEASHES, TOYS)
Campbell Pet Company
http://www.campbellpet.com/

J-B Wholesale Pet Supplies
http://www.jbpet.com/

J and J Dog Supplies
http://www.jjdog.com/

KONG® Company
http://www.kongcompany.com/

Lupine® Pet
http://www.lupine.com/

Nylabone®
http://www.nylabone.com/

Petedge
http://www.petedge.com/

Premier® Pet Products
http://www.gentleleader.com/

Proactive Pet
http://www.proactivepet.com/

Puppy Playground
http://www.puppyplayground.com/

PLAYGROUND EQUIPMENT
Puppy Playground
http://www.puppyplayground.com/

SOFTWARE APPLICATIONS FOR DOG DAYCARES
Kennel Connection
http://www.kennelconnection.com/

Kennel Link
http://kennellink.com/

KennelSoft
http://www.kennelsoft.com/

SOUND DEADENING
B-Quiet
http://www.b-quiet.com/

Occupational Safety and Health
http://www.osha.gov/SLTC/noisehearingconservation/

TRADE ASSOCIATIONS AND GROUPS
American Boarding Kennel Association (ABKA)
http://www.abka.com/
A non-profit trade association for pet care service businesses. Is working toward the establishment of daycare industry standards and voluntary accreditation of facilities

American Veterinary Medical Association (AVMA)
http://www.avma.org/
A non-profit trade associations for the veterinary profession

Association of Pet Dog Trainers (APDT)
http://www.apdt.com/
A professional organization of trainers committed to better training through education

Daycare lists at Yahoogroups
Visit   http://groups.yahoo.com/   and   search   for   either dogdaycare   or   nadda   (or   both).   Join   the   lists   using   the information provided

WEBCAMS
Online Doggie
http://www.onlinedoggie.com

Index

About the Author

Robin K. Bennett, CPDT is the owner of All About Dogs, Inc., the largest dog-training facility in Northern Virginia. She started her company in 1993 doing private obedience classes in owner's homes. She has since extended her business to include several family pet dog training classes, behavior modification lessons, and temperament evaluations.

Robin successfully owned and operated her own dog daycare for many years and is a dog daycare consultant. She is a national speaker and has presented seminars on dog daycare and playgroup matters for several organizations including the Association of Pet Dog Trainers, the American Boarding Kennel Association, Groom Classic, Groom Expo and the Pet Services Expo.

Robin has an excellent working relationship with local veterinarians as well as the Prince William Animal Control Bureau. She has been recommended by both groups to evaluate potentially dangerous dogs. She is an active member of the Association of Pet Dog Trainers, and has a B.A. degree from Roanoke College. Robin regularly attends dog training seminars, and has earned Level 1 certification through the Certification Council for Pet Dog Trainers (CCPDT), the first national certification for dog trainers.

Robin lives in Stafford, Virginia with her husband, Greg; their children, Leanna and Nathan; and two dogs, Carrie and Denver. When she's not dealing with dogs, Robin is a Lieutenant Colonel in the United States Marine Corps Reserve.